A Treasure Hunting Text

Ram Publications
Hal Dawson, Editor

Let's Talk Treasure Hunting
The ultimate "how-to" book of treasure hunting — with or without a metal detector; describes all kinds of treasures and tells how to find them.

The New Successful Coin Hunting
The world's most authoritative guide to finding valuable coins, totally rewritten to include instructions for 21st Century detectors.

Treasure Recovery from Sand and Sea
Step-by-step instructions for reaching the "blanket of wealth" beneath sands nearby and under the world's waters, totally rewritten for the 90's.

Modern Electronic Prospecting
Explains in layman's terms how to use a modern detector to find gold nuggets and veins; includes instructions for panning and dredging.

Modern Metal Detectors
Comprehensive guide to all types of metal detectors; designed to increase understanding and expertise about all aspects of these electronic marvels.

Gold Panning is Easy
Excellent new field guide shows the beginner exactly how to find and pan gold; follow these instructions and perform as well as any professional.

Weekend Prospecting
Offers simple "how-to" instructions for enjoying holidays and vacations profitably by prospecting with metal detectors and gold pans.

Treasure Hunting Pays Off
A basic introduction to all facets of treasure hunting...the equipment, targets and terminology; totally revised for 21st Century detectors.

Buried Treasures You Can Find
Complete field guide for finding treasure; includes state-by-state listing of thousands of sites where treasure is believed to exist.

Treasure from British Waters
One of Great Britain's best known detector hobbyists tells how and where to find treasure in the waters of England and the Balearic Islands.

Sunken Treasure: How to Find It
One of the world's foremost underwater salvors shares a lifetime's experience in locating and recovering treasure from deep beneath the sea.

True Treasure Tales -- Gar Starrett Adventures
The Secret of John Murrell's Vault
The Missing Nez Perce Gold

Real Gold
in those Golden Years

By Charles Garrett
Let Metal Detecting Enrich Your Life

ISBN 0-915920-78-6
Library of Congress Catalog Card No. 94-67196
Real Gold in Those Golden Years
Copyright 1994
Charles Garrett

First Printing, October 1995

Book and cover design by Mel Climer

For FREE listing of treasure hunting books write

Ram Publishing Company

P.O. Box 38649   •   Dallas, TX 75238

Real Gold in Those Golden Years...

Contents

By Charles Garrett

Treasure Hunting Texts

Let's Talk Treasure Hunting
Treasure Recovery from Sand and Sea
The New Successful Coin Hunting
The New Modern Metal Detectors
Treasure Hunting Pays Off
Treasure Hunting Secrets

With Roy Lagal

Modern Treasure Hunting
Modern Electronic Prospecting

True Treasure Tales

The Secret of John Murrell's Vault
The Missing Nez Perce Gold

From the Editor

H e ain't heavy. He's m'brother...so goes the famous caption. Similarly, this book was never "heavy" because it is a real labor of love for both Charles Garrett and for me. We love the subject matter — metal detecting — and we truly believe in this book's premise...that the hobby will enrich the lives of all who pursue it.

Also, when we talk about "the golden years," both Charles and I speak from experience. Though it's hard for us to realize, we've both passed the three-score mark in age. Plus, we each have friends, older as well as younger, who could benefit from the message of this book.

These friends have succeeded in the business and professional world, some beyond their wildest dreams. Yet, their so-called golden years appear to be lacking. Charles knows how much metal detecting has meant to him and to countless others. Both he and I are confident that this hobby can bring the same pleasures and thrills — indeed, a youthful sense of anticipation and adventure — to the life of anyone who will walk with a detector and listen for the sound of treasure.

The name of Charles Garrett ranks high on any list of those men and women who have pioneered the development and use of metal detectors...whether for discovery of treasure...for security...or, for any other reason. Charles did not set out to become a leading manufacturer of metal detection equipment. He prepared himself well, however, to become one of the world's foremost treasure hunters. Since boyhood he has been enthralled with stories of hidden wealth...tales which brought excitement to his semi-rural youth in the Piney Woods of Deep East Texas. Throughout his life he has continually sought to learn all that he could about techniques and equipment for treasure hunting.

After graduation from Lufkin (Texas) High School and service in the U.S. Navy during the Korean conflict, he earned a degree in electrical engineering from Lamar University in Beaumont and began his business career in Dallas with Texas Instruments and Teledyne Geotech.

Some three decades ago, then, Charles was a young electrical engineer deeply engrossed in development of systems and equipment required by America's fledgling space effort. In devoting himself to his lifetime hobby of treasure hunting, however, he also designed and built metal detectors in his spare time. Because his detectors were obviously more effective than any available commercially, they became popular with fellow treasure hunters for whom he was soon making them. This avocation became a career when he founded Garrett Electronics to produce his inventions.

Today, the name Garrett stands as a synonym for the treasure hunting metal detector. Charles himself is known as the *Grand Master Hunter,* also the name of his company's first computerized instrument, described at the time as "the finest metal detector ever manufactured." Garrett detectors have discovered some of the world's great treasures.

His Company is also the world's foremost manufacturer of security metal detection equipment. Not only do its famed Magnascanner and Super Scanner instruments protect schools, courtrooms and air travelers, but they have been honored as the choice to safeguard historical and cultural treasures, Olympic athletes, presidents and kings.

He is married to the former Eleanor Smith of Pennington, TX, who has played a key role in the growth of Garrett Electronics. They have two sons and a daughter.

As a graduate engineer and a businessman, Charles introduced discipline to the manufacture of metal detectors. He has generally raised the standards of metal detecting everywhere, while the hobby has grown from a haphazard pastime to almost a science.

Garrett quality is known throughout the world. From the beginning, Charles Garrett vowed "to practice what I preach" — in other words, to test his equipment in the field...to insure that it will *work* for customers regardless of ground conditions and environment. Thus, with a metal detector of his own design he has searched for and found treasure on every continent except Antarctica. He has also scanned under lakes, seas and oceans of the world. In addition, he is the foremost author in the field of metal detection, with numerous books, articles and technical papers.

He already considers this book one of his all-time favorites, however, because of the people for whom it is intended.

Hal Dawson
Editor, Ram Publishing

Dallas, Texas
Summer 1994

Charles Garrett

By Charles Garrett...

Author's Note

Treasure hunting with a metal detector is the finest hobby in the world...for men and women of any age! I'm convinced of that, and I should know because I've been using a detector to find coins, relics and other valuable and interesting items for almost half a century now. Yet, even on those occasions when I haven't found much of anything — and, believe me, there have been plenty — I had a good time. I enjoyed the thrill of a search. I remained excited about what I was *about* to find. I was often with delightful companions. Plus, I benefited from the exercise and fresh air that this glorious hobby "forced" on me.

If you appreciate the outdoors but don't like exercise, get a metal detector. When you're hunting with it, you'll enjoy the outdoors as never before and scarcely realize the healthy exercise that you're getting for yourself (that you probably could use anyway).

Hunting with a metal detector is a wonderful hobby for anyone. But, it's especially good for those of us approaching what are sometimes called *The Golden Years*...the years of slowing down a bit...the years of relaxing...the years of enjoying the pleasures of life without all the day-to-day pressures.

Yet, for many the years of retirement are far from golden. They're downright boring and sometimes frightening. Yes, frightening, because there's nothing worse for a busy person than to have *nothing to do*. Now, doing nothing may sound idyllic, but it can be a prescription for slow death. Boredom is a disease that can kill. I know because I've seen it happen...a dynamic individual leaves his or her business or profession and sets out to "enjoy life." But, this man or woman faces a bigger challenge than ever encountered before...finding something to do! Without that "something" to make it worthwhile and enjoyable, life becomes agony and the "Golden Years" can soon become tarnished beyond hope of recovery.

This book discusses frankly the potential problems faced by someone with "nothing to do." Plus, it offers a simple suggestion for avoiding such an impasse: consider the hobby of metal detecting as your "something to do."

I'm always amazed that some people simply refuse to experience the marvelous pleasures and thrills of hunting with a metal detector. And, I often ask them, "Why?"

"Oh, a really good metal detector is too complicated," they explain..."too expensive...I don't travel, you see...my health won't permit anything strenuous...it's just not the sort of thing I would do."

Rubbish!

Metal detecting no longer need be complicated or expensive, and it's the ideal hobby for persons of any physical condition. Hunt as little or as much as you like; you decide just how strenuous you want your hobby to be. And, while it absolutely doesn't require travel, this fascinating hobby can certainly add a new and exciting dimension to any occasional journey. As for not being "something I would do"...how do you know unless you've tried it?

Any time, virtually any place...you *can* eventually find treasure with a modern metal detector. Take my word for it!

This book will teach you the basics for using a modern metal detector effectively — and, incidentally, how to find treasure. Not treasure buried far away...in another city...another state...another land, but treasure buried literally in your own back yard.

Who can find this lost wealth? Practically anyone...male or female, an individual searching almost full time or only occasionally. Sometimes this effort will be scarcely more than walking down a beautiful and sunny beach.

You can search for a few minutes now and then or do it daily for the rest of your life. Coins in a park...jewelry on the beach...gold nuggets in a mountain stream...nostalgic relics lost in a ghost town...a buried money cache. Any of these may be *your* treasure, and this book will tell you exactly how to find it while you enrich your life and realize the promise of your golden years. Let them become *really* golden!

And, the hobby of metal detecting offers so many opportunities for fellowship and service. I have gained great personal satisfaction from developing and working in programs that allow handicapped children to experience the thrill of finding treasure. Similar opportunities to enrich your life by bringing pleasure to others await you.

This book is not a metal detector instruction manual. Instead, it will try to reveal how you can improve your life and enjoy it more thoroughly. Simple instructions will be presented that will take you to the very heart of treasure hunting...you will learn how just a little research and field searching can result in the excitement of finding instant wealth...and, finding it buried at your very feet.

Man and boy, I've spent almost five decades hunting treasure, and some have said that I'm good at it. I'll offer no opinion except to say that I believe I've found more than my share.

Basically, however, my life has been spent developing search and recovery skills that others did not know or were not willing to take the necessary time to learn. And, that's what this book is about...sharing my skills and techniques to help you perfect your abilities while you pursue the fascinating hobby of metal detecting...a hobby that can not only pay for itself but can prove *very* rewarding.

Simply stated, I want you to get more out of your life by learning about the hobby of metal detecting.

Maybe your goal has always been a "grand treasure," one

you must spend considerable time researching and recovering, or perhaps you just want an interesting new hobby that will let you enjoy yourself while finding pocket change in the park...on a beach...or anywhere else. Either way, this book will offer simple instructions and suggestions to guide you as you enter the enchanting world of metal detecting.

Heed this warning before you start: once you discover your first "treasure" — be it a simple one-cent coin, a valuable ring or even a gold nugget — you risk becoming hooked on metal detecting. You'll wonder why you waited so darn long to take up the hobby.

I predict...you'll love it!

Charles Garrett

Garland, Texas
Summer 1994

Chapter 1 — *A Grand and Glorious Hobby...*
Metal Detecting

The appeal of hunting with a metal detector is universal. The desire to seek and find hidden wealth is as old as mankind. It transcends all boundaries of age, sex, personality and social status. Furthermore, this hobby offers opportunities to older individuals that can be matched by no other.

This book then is all about the pleasure that can come from using a modern metal detector. Moreover, the book is especially written for older men and women who have never tried the hobby. Whether you picked up this book yourself or had it handed to you by a friend or relative, I urge that you at least scan it. The hobby of metal detecting may change your life. The *Real Gold* mentioned in its title might turn out to be a treasure found by your detector. Even more importantly, it could prove to be a genuine enrichment of your life made possible by this new hobby...no matter what treasures you might find. Just remember that metal detecting is a delightful hobby that often will pay for itself!

Treasure hunting with a metal detector is difficult to define because it can mean so many different things. Basically, it is the search for and recovery of anything that *you* consider valuable. That's right, only you can determine what's treasure and what's not. Coins, costume jewelry, money caches and relics are all treasure just the same as gold and jewels or whatever else you are looking for.

No matter what the target, metal detecting is an absolutely universal outdoor hobby! Anyone can hunt for treasure with equal intensity anywhere on the face of the earth or under its

9

waters. Each individual decides how much energy is required for participation in the hobby, and the decision can be changed from day to day or even from one minute to the next. The hobbyist can hunt for hours a day or for just a short while; the hunting may be strenuous or involve little exertion.

Treasure hunting sites are equally optional. While hidden wealth can be sought at exotic foreign locations, many successful hobbyists swear that the ideal hunting ground is one's own back yard or neighborhood.

Treasure hunting with a metal detector simply adds a modern wrinkle to an accepted ancient pastime. Some people want (or, expect) to strike it rich the very first time they turn on a detector, while others are content to find little more than a few coins in the local park. Some individuals hunt with a detector for the excitement of digging a treasure out of the ground, while others are fascinated by the "historical" discoveries they make. Some delight in returning lost class rings and other valuables to their rightful owners. Others enjoy displaying in their homes the treasures they have discovered. Yet, some simply appreciate another opportunity for getting out into the great outdoors. Any treasure they find is icing on the cake.

Treasure hunting is an ideal hobby for mature men and women — yes, senior citizens — whose health permits (or requires) light outdoor exercise. Equally as important to the older generation can be the aura of adventure this hobby will bring to otherwise placid lives. Treasure hunting generates an opportunity for excitement and suspense without requiring the rigors or expense of lengthy travel and elaborate equipment.

New-found treasure brings joy into the life of anyone, but the pleasures of metal detecting go far beyond simply those of acquiring wealth.

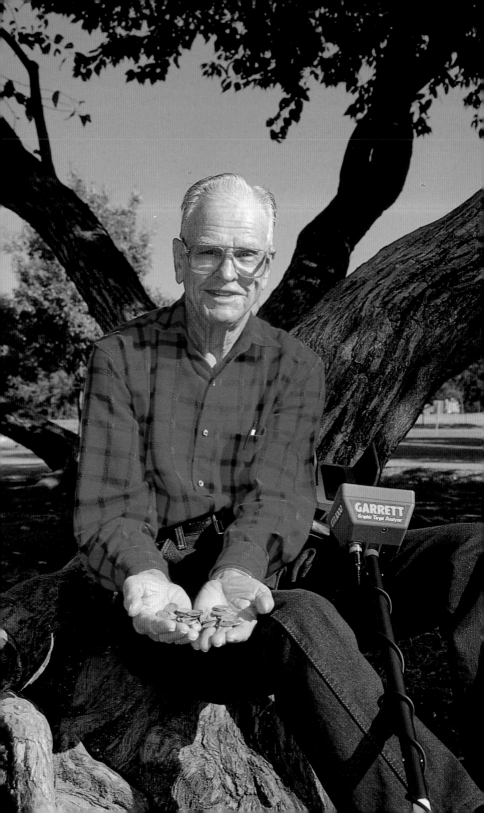

Truly, hunting with a metal detector fascinates everyone. You just can never know what you might expect to find. And, it is a hobby that can literally pay for itself since it offers financial rewards as well as the benefits of healthy exercise and outdoor activity. Finally, no matter what a person's age, health, financial status or social standing...nothing can compare with the sheer thrill of discovery — whether it be that first coin...a ring...a gold nugget...an outlaw cache. The joy and excitement enrich both the spirit and the pocketbook.

This *Treasure Hunting Text* provides basic information on the initial use of a metal detector — the research required to select targets as well as the techniques for recovering them. Moreover, it will explain the operation of appropriate modern detectors.

If you're interested in what a metal detector can find, you're probably an inquisitive person by nature...and have been one all your life. You've always wanted to discover what's just over the horizon...around the next bend...or, under the next layer of soil. If so, great success in hunting with a metal detector can be yours... especially if you use a quality instrument. All you need now is a little knowledge.

First, learn about your metal detector — its searchcoils, accessories, modes of operation and capabilities. Put your study into action with practice, especially in the field. But, even if you hunt only occasionally, you can have success with a modern one-touch metal detector. They're so easy to use!

Treasure hunting has become a family hobby...husband, wife and children all become dedicated treasure hunters. Sometimes only the man of the household enjoys the hobby, but I know of some wives who will go hunting alone when

There are those who have become so proficient at the hobby of metal detecting that they can expand their interests into coin collecting or other areas.

the husband can't go. Often, children become more proficient than their parents or grandparents. Hunters, fishermen, campers, vacationers and backpackers are adding metal detectors to their sports gear.

Treasure hunting is healthful!

Who can deny that outdoor activities are healthful? Treasure hunting certainly takes you out of doors into the fresh air and sunshine. Scanning a detector over the ground, stooping to dig targets, hiking into new areas...all of this can stimulate the heart and lungs while putting new demands on unused muscles. But, this is where an extra side benefit is realized. A "built-in" body maintenance program is a valuable *plus* of treasure hunting. Leg muscles stay firm, flab around the middle may diminish, breathing improves and nights of restful sleep foretell a longer, healthier life.

Metal detecting can be profitable!

It is also simple and easy. Why not begin by considering the hobby of coin hunting? The majority of all detector owners begin their new hobby by hunting for coins. Countless millions of coins have been lost and await recovery by the metal detector hobbyist. More coins are being lost every day than are being found...and this has been going on for centuries!

Many persons who begin by scanning with their detectors only for coins often extend their hobby into other areas of treasure hunting. Searching ghost towns and old houses for hidden money caches, and hunting in trash dumps for relics and rare bottles can be very rewarding. One treasure hunter found $41,000 in currency in a metal box that was cached in an old dumping ground. Another man in Idaho found a $20 gold piece estimated to be worth hundreds of thousands of dollars. Countless small fruit jar and "post hole" money caches are uncovered each year.

Most important to many people is the awareness and enjoyment of treasures of nature that have been placed upon the earth for all of us to find. Whether a treasure of monetary

14

value can be found is never really the point. It is truly gratifying to see nature in its purest form all around and to be a vital part of it. This alone could well be the greatest treasure.

Educational factors related to treasure hunting can be equally stimulating. Relics and artifacts of bygone eras raise many questions. What happened to the people who lived and prospered where only faint traces remain to mark the existence of a once-thriving city or town? Why was the area left deserted? These and other mysteries can usually be solved with proper research and examination of the artifacts found.

Research

Many find it amazing that the successful hobbyist appears to remain fresh and eager, while other who use metal detectors seem to run about constantly in a helter-skelter fashion, chasing some sort of will-o-the-wisp...never being really satisfied or successful.

To get the most from this hobby you will want to hunt correctly and in the right places. Most good discoveries result from research. Whether you hunt in the park or on the beach...whether you are a coin hunter, cache or relic hunter, or a prospector, research is important. It is a basic tool you cannot neglect to use if you want to enjoy success.

Always remember that if you decide to find treasure, you must go where it is located. You can't find treasure where it is not present; you will find treasure where it is! Most of the time, to find where a treasure is located, you should carry out a certain amount of research. You will want to study, read and follow up leads. It's wise to talk to people. In short, do your research. But then, folks our age have done a lot of research by just living. Think back on your past. Don't you know where something might be that a metal detector could locate? Follow "treasure leads" that nobody else knows about!

Living the Hobby

For the hobbyist who takes pride in his or her efforts the greatest difficulty is deciding which of the dozens or hundreds of leads to follow. The common sense that comes with age and experience is a big factor in metal detecting just as it is in any other human activity.

Many successful hobbyists seem to live and breathe the hobby. It is always on his or her mind. Consequently, every-thing that person reads and everyone they talk with are potential sources of the fresh treasure leads and data they need to help in their work.

If you are a coin hunter, for instance, you can find current coins all day long at the park, playground and along grassy strips near parking meters. If you really want to start finding old and rare, valuable coins, however, you might want to undertake some research. Learn where the old settlers' campgrounds, carnival and fairground sites are located. (Maybe you already know; maybe you were there!) These are the valuable hot spots; here you will find treasure that makes hunting profitable. This same principle applies to any other kind of searching.

If you are looking for gold, it's best to hunt where precious metal has already been found, especially if you're a novice. Virgin territory still exists, especially in arid areas where no water is available for ore processing Yet, you can find gold and silver in thousands of locations throughout the world where the metals have been mined. Relic and cache hunters must also do their research. Find the hot spots, then use the detector knowledge you are gaining. It will pay off!

To find treasure you must prepare yourself with the right attitude. Now, you know that this requires some research — but, at the same time, you need to get busy...get outdoors and into the field. How hard you hunt, what hours you keep...all of this is strictly up to you.

The hobby is a grand and glorious one for so many people I have known over the past half-century. I can only wish that you will find the same joy that they — and I — have experienced.

Chapter 2 — For Those Growing Older...

An Ideal Hobby

Most people seem to believe that old age is 10 years older than you are right now. Yet none of us has any choice about growing old; it's a fact of life. In preparing this book I researched to some extent the literature of aging and was pleasantly surprised at the volume and quality of material I found. And, no matter what I read, I had to agree with one author who observed that there is nothing particularly wonderful about growing old. It just happens. But, if you ever become concerned about any problem associated with aging, just visit your nearest library or a good bookstore. You'll be amazed by the numerous solutions suggested for any of your problems, both real and imagined. Of course, I was especially gratified to discover how well the hobby of metal detecting fits easily and realistically into so much of the good advice offered to aging individuals.

Older people today are healthier, better off financially and live longer than ever before. They are also better educated and more independent, both in spirit and lifestyle.

Now is the most exciting time to be growing old that the world has ever seen! There is a tremendous surge in knowledge about the aging process, and the enormous increase of older people in the population is affecting how society views the elderly and those growing old.

We are in the midst of a population explosion among the aged. More people are living longer than ever before. As recently as 1960 the death rate at age 65 was 25 deaths for every 1,000 persons. Today fewer than 20 people out of a thousand die in their 65th year, a 20% drop since 1960.

Charles Garrett

Right now, more than half of all the human beings in the world who ever reached the age of 65 are still alive. Just imagine! During the next century when the children of the Baby Boom generation reach their 50s, more than 100 million older Americans are expected to populate our nation. Meanwhile, life should continue to lengthen for the average person. Being old is increasingly more a state of mind than a chronological or biological marker.

After 60 are we on a steep downgrade mentally? Don't you believe it! Age is no barrier to learning, and universities around the world open their doors and welcome older people. The myth that old people cannot learn new things is just that — a myth. Today, older people are learning astrophysics, digital electronics and modern business methods. And, that is only with the left hemisphere of the brain. With the right hemisphere they are learning to paint with water colors, to arrange flowers and to make ceramics. Learning to find lots of treasure with a simple one-touch metal detector is a snap!

Variety, excitement, expectation, adventure...within limits — each of these is proposed as a prescription for living a more satisfying and longer life. Now, the methods for filling these prescriptions, depending on physical capabilities, budget requirements and individual interests, can be varied — to say the least! That's why you'll find so many books and articles written about growing older successfully.

I hope you will agree that the hobby of metal detecting fulfills many of the suggestions usually offered for a happier and more meaningful life. Now, I'll admit that I'm prejudiced. Yet, let's consider some of the prescriptions for happiness ordinarily given to older people:

Put variety into your life is a common recommendation, followed by numerous suggestions — some of them rather outlandish — for achieving this variety. These proposals make me shake my head and chuckle. What greater variety is there to be found than by listening to a metal detector and digging up all that it finds!

It's an accepted fact that unless you are stimulated...unless you are challenged, your mind will stagnate. I'm not talking about artificial simulation with any of the fancy so-called "therapies." I recommend something practical and obvious like metal detecting to set your mind to working again.

Create excitement is another common bit of advice, usually accompanied by some rather bizarre suggestions. Once again, I merely smile and think of the excitement I experience every time my metal detector finds a target!

Look forward to something, we are told...have a sense of the future. Many studies have shown the value of keeping a fix on the future as a means of maintaining mental health. It figures, of course, that people who look forward must have a sound sense of themselves and their place in the world. When my detector sounds off on a target, I certainly know where I am. And, you can bet I'm looking forward...to digging up what my detector has found. Wouldn't you? I'm also looking forward whenever I research a long-lost cache. I can't wait for the day I am able to seek it with a detector.

Summing all of this up is generally the advice that older men and women *find adventure*. Easier said than done for most of us! Yet, treasure hunting with a metal detector *provides all the adventure that I need*. It offers the armchair sort of adventure which comes from reading about treasure hunting and researching the locations of buried wealth. Then, I can decide how much more adventure I want (or need) by looking for it with my detector. Believe me, if you will hunt actively with a metal detector, *adventure will seek you out!*

It has been said that a person's life naturally divides itself into three segments...the *learning* years, zero to 25; the *earning* years, 25 to 50; and the *living* years that follow. This is well put because statistics on modern aging tell us today that we can expect to live one-third of our lives after age 50.

During our working years, the need for an adequately stimulating life is likely to take care of itself. Having a job and raising a family are challenges that force us to use our brains continually. But, as we reach retirement age, we may be forced to exercise our mental muscles less often. Thus, we must actively seek out an enriched outer life. If we allow our interest in the world and living to erode greatly, we must expect to pay a price. Not only may we seem less intelligent, our brain itself may actually change.

Each man or woman of any age needs a good reason for meeting the day with vigor and expectation. Goals lend direction and vitality to the person pursuing them. A day with no goal, not even the goal of creative loafing, is condemned to be a day of aging and nothing else. A life without goals is, by definition, no life at all.

During our years of "learning" and "earning," most worthwhile goals are thrust upon us by mentors, business conditions and similar situations. We accept good goals without even thinking about them. During our years of "living," it is less likely that worthwhile goals will be "thrust upon us." Time forces us to take our fate into our own hands.

Middle-age is the prime time to plan for a happy old age. It is to old age as childhood is to adolescence and adolescence is to adulthood. The middle years should be a time of looking ahead and preparing — preparing an environment and a way of life that will provide opportunities for satisfying activities — ones that are conducive to self-respect.

I've heard it said that the goal of every man or woman should be to die young...at the oldest age possible! Does a "fountain of youth" exist? Of course it does — it is inside each of us! Only, not everyone knows how to find it. I propose that you permit the hobby of metal detecting to help you discover your own fountain of youth.

No matter what preconceived notions you might have about this hobby I urge you to approach the subject with an open mind. I can't help but think of a gentleman from Virginia who visited our factory a few years ago. When he retired years earlier after a long and distinguished career in government service, one of his sons had given him a new Garrett metal detector. Now, the son was an avid detector hobbyist. He knew how much he enjoyed hunting for and finding treasure, and he hoped that his father, now that he had time on his hands, might also grow to love the hobby. Yet, the older man told me that he was truly appalled by the gift and considered it almost an insult. "It's funny now," he commented, "but I somehow didn't consider metal detecting a gentleman's hobby. From what I knew about 'treasure hunting,' I felt that it was somehow beneath my station in life."

Fortunately for this individual, his intelligence and curiosity overcame his false pride. After reading the Owner's Manual that accompanied his detector, he became intrigued with the possibilities of his new instrument and tentatively tried to use it. As a modern detector, it was effective as well as easy to understand. As an intelligent man, he was quickly able to hunt with it properly. Of course, he began finding coins immediately. Living in the midst of Civil War battlefields, he soon expanded his interest into relics. Those of us who use a metal detector know what happened next. He was hooked for life!

Our meeting came when this gentlemen made a special effort to visit the Garrett factory so that he could thank me personally for the years of joy that metal detecting had already brought into his life. He also proudly displayed some of his finds and wanted information on our newer models.

Such visits from satisfied customers of all ages are not rarities at the Garrett factory. It's a real pleasure for us to respond to the gratitude of these customers who are our friends and to try to answer their questions. In fact, one of the few complaints that I have about my life today would be that I simply don't have enough time to spend with people such as these. Yet I try! I sincerely hope that you will let me make time for you soon!

Charles Garrett

Understanding Detectors

P ress one touchpad. Begin finding treasure immediately. And, you may *never* have to touch another control. It's that easy to use and understand a modern metal detector!

I've been finding all sorts of things with these instruments for more than 30 years, and I'm still amazed at the ease with which new models can be operated. In fact, the modern one-touch detectors are so simple that it's sometimes uncanny. Metal detectors generally are incredibly easier to hunt with today than they were when I first began trying to find treasure with a war surplus U.S. Army mine detector.

Plus, modern computerized circuitry will find *more* treasure and will find it quicker and easier. Over the years I've participated (led the way, some might say) in the continuing improvements as they have been made in detector circuitry and design. Year by year we steadily improved all of our instruments. But, the advancements made by the Garrett Engineering Lab in just the past few years have been truly breathtaking. You see, the metal detector has entered the computer age, and treasure hunting has never been simpler than with a computerized one-touch detector.

It's not necessary to understand the scientific principles of metal detection to hunt with a detector. Press a touchpad, and you can find coins, rings, jewelry, gold nuggets, caches or whatever you are searching for without understanding how your detector is operating. But. it's been my observation that men and women our age have a little more interest in just what makes things tick than younger folks.

It's always helpful to remember that a good metal detector will never lie; it will simply report what's lying beneath its searchcoil. Thus, successful hobbyists find it helpful to know just how a metal detector goes about finding metal and telling them what it has found.

To understand what a metal detector is and how it operates we need to know just what it is *not*. A detector is not an instrument (Geiger counter) that detects energy emissions from radioactive materials. It is not an instrument (magnetometer) that measures the intensity of magnetic fields. It will never "point" to coins, jewelry or any other kind of metal; it does not attempt to measure the abundance of metal. A metal detector is simply an instrument that *detects* the presence of metal and *reports* its discoveries through audible and visible signals.

When a coin or other treasure is made of metal — and, most of them usually are — a metal detector can signal their location a reasonable distance beneath its searchcoil. How all this comes about is somewhat more complicated.

Every type of metal detector detects metal essentially by the transmission and reception of radio wave signals. This is basic: when a detector is turned on, a radio signal is transmitted from the searchcoil, generating an electromagnetic field that flows out into any surrounding medium, whether it be earth, rock, water, wood, air or what-have-you. Electromagnetic field lines penetrate metal whenever it comes within the detection path. The extent of this detection depends upon the power used to transmit the signal and the resistance of the medium into which the signal is transmitted.

The electromagnetic field generated by the searchcoil's transmission causes something called *eddy currents* to flow on the surface of metal detected by this field. Because generation of these currents on the metal results in loss of power in the electromagnetic field, this loss of power is immediately sensed by the detector's circuitry.

And, simultaneously, a secondary electromagnetic field is generated by the eddy currents into the surrounding medium. The primary electromagnetic field of the detector is further disturbed by electromagnetic field lines passing through certain metals.

These currents and the resulting distortion of the electromagnetic field itself are all sensed by a metal detector. A receiver in the searchcoil detects both the secondary field and the distorted primary field at the same time the loss of generating power is being noted by the instrument. Circuitry of the metal detector simultaneously interprets all of the sensations so that appropriate signals can be provided for the operator. A detector will report instantly whenever some sort of metallic object appears to be present. Good metal detectors can even measure the conductivity of the electromagnetic currents to determine what kind of metal is present.

Quite simply, the quality of signals generated, received and interpreted by the metal detector and the ability of the treasure hunter to act upon them determine the difference between "digging junk" and finding treasure.

When you begin studying mineralization, target identification, field applications and other subjects, you'll be glad you learned this background material. It will help you to understand what your detector is telling you...why you hear certain signals. You will become better able to determine if the object you have detected is one that you want to dig. Proper and highly efficient operation of a modern metal detector is not difficult. Press one touchpad and you can find treasure. Believe me! Greatest success in the hobby, however, requires a certain amount of study, thought and field application.

Depth of Detection

How deep can a metal detector find metal? When an electromagnetic field flows out of its searchcoil, three factors determine whether detection is possible: electromagnetic

25

field strength, target size and surface area of the target. How far the electromagnetic field flows from the searchcoil also depends on the size of the searchcoil and materials that are present in the earth. Larger searchcoils produce larger fields that can probe more deeply.

It is realistic to expect that a coin-sized target can be detected at depths to six or nine inches. Yet, sometimes detection is inches deeper and, sometimes, shallower...all because of such variables as ground mineralization, atmospheric conditions and the conductivity of the metal in the target itself. Orientation of the target can have an effect on depth of detection.

Surface Area

Generally speaking, modern metal detectors are surface area detectors. They are not metallic volume (mass) detectors. How a detector "sees" a target will be determined to a large extent by the surface area of a metal target that is "looking at" the bottom of the searchcoil. You can prove for yourself that the actual volume or mass of a target has very little to do with most forms of detection.

Lay your detector down and turn it on. Now move a large coin toward the searchcoil with the face of the coin "looking at" the bottom of the coil. Note how far away the coin is detected. Next, move the coin back and turn it so that the narrow edge "looks at" the searchcoil's bottom. You will notice that when it is turned this way, the coin must come closer to the searchcoil to be detected. The mass of metal itself did not change, only the surface area of the coin facing the searchcoil.

Another proof is to measure the distance a single coin can be detected. Then, stack several coins on the back side of the test coin and check to see how far this stack of coins can be detected. You'll find that the stack can be detected at only a slightly greater distance when the face of only one coin faces the searchcoil, illustrating that the larger volume of metal had very little effect on detection distance.

26

Fringe-area detection is a characteristic whose under-standing will enable you to detect metal targets to the maximum depth capability of any instrument. The normal detection pattern for a coin may extend, say, nine inches below the searchcoil; the detection pattern for a small jar of coins may extend perhaps 18 inches. Within these areas of detection your detector will sound an unmistakable audio signal of discovery.

But detection is also taking place outside the detection pattern. Signals from this detection, however, are too weak to be heard by the operator except in the fringe area directly adjacent to the outer edges of the normal detection pattern.

Wear Headphones

The ability to hear fringe-area signals results in greatly improved metal detection efficiency and success. If you want to hear such signals, a good set of headphones is a must, along with training yourself in the art of discerning those faint whispers of sound that can signal the presence of a target in your fringe area. You can develop the ability to hear these signals with practice, training, concentration and faith in your detector and its ability. Those of you who develop fringe area detection capability will discover treasures that other hob-byists miss.

Combine this capability by using a modern computerized instrument that can detect deeper and more precisely, and you're part of a treasure hunting team that can't be beat!

How Detectors "Report"

When a treasure hunter is scanning his searchcoil over the ground or in the water, a detector reports information on targets in three ways:

• Increases or decreases in audible volume (universal on all detectors);

• Graphic information presented on LCD meters (some-times reported in a numerical "code");

• Meter deflections (types of meters can vary greatly, along with the amount and accuracy of the information they present).

Acceptable objects cause the audio or visual indicators to increase in amplitude; unacceptable objects cause the indicators to decrease. Metered target identification indicators can provide additional information concerning the possible "value" of targets.

Good targets will generally be announced by a clear and distinct tone while the detector will produce "blip-like" sounds for pulltabs and similar small trash.

Learn to listen closely to your detector's signals, and interpret what it is "telling" you through sound and meter/LCD indicators. You'll be glad you did because you'll find more treasure!

Over

Control panels of the Garrett GTA 350 (top) and CX III indicate how simple these detectors are to use with their touchpads and graphic instructions.

Facing

Metal detecting has involved the author in interesting and unusual situations such as this historic expedition that traced the route of the Biblical Exodus .

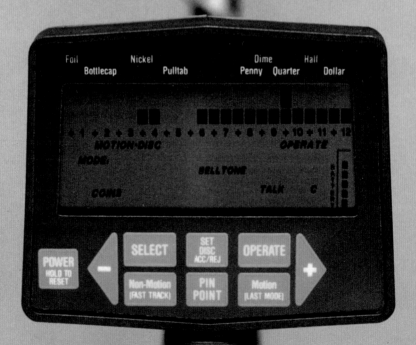

Choosing Your Detector

This will probably be the most important chapter of the book for most of you. I want to offer some tips on selecting the right detector. And, unless you get that *right* detector, you aren't going to enjoy the hobby. I also want to explain a bit about the economics of metal detecting...to tell you why this can be such a relatively inexpensive hobby.

Since this question of affordability is one that many of you want answered even before you consider the hobby, let's look at it first. Perhaps you've heard that metal detectors are expensive. Well, they do cost more than a lot of other hobby-type items. There's no question about that. But, remember, you must have a quality detector to appreciate the hobby, and

Over

Metal detecting has enabled Charles Garrett to associate with scores of delightful individuals such as this "grizzled" prospector, Rattlesnake John.

Facing

This retired Air Force officer has chosen the Garrett Sea Hunter, and his wife has selected the Master Hunter CX for beach hunting in Florida.

we're talking about the *one-time* purchase of a scientific, electronic instrument.

Concerning dollars and cents, however, please don't make the very common mistake of thinking that you must choose the highest priced detector to get the best instrument...or, think that you must have the fanciest detector to get the most out of the hobby. Even if you can afford it, you may find yourself with one that's so complicated that you'll spend more time adjusting controls and loading programs than treasure hunting!

Remember, you're looking for value. That means the most detector for the dollar.

So, instead of buying the most expensive (or the lowest price, for that matter) instrument, determine a price *range* that fits your pocketbook. Then, diligently analyze all detectors priced within that range before buying the one that suits you best and measures up to the standards of quality and value you will determine from studying this book.

Another suggestion that I'll offer is that you decide just exactly what features you want in a detector. Then, try to find as many of them as possible in a detector that fits your pocketbook. I guess I'm recommending that you try to set a balance between what you need and how much you have to pay for it. Let me urge you, however, not to compromise and buy a detector without features you feel you must have. Remember, if you buy something you don't like, it will be hard to fall in love with it later.

How much should you spend for a detector? Remember that you generally get what you pay for. Because a quality metal detector is a scientific instrument, you shouldn't expect it to be inexpensive. In fact, starting out with a cheap detector is a sure-fire way to shorten your detecting career. You'll quit in a hurry because you won't find anything.

And, unfortunately, you'll probably tell people, "Oh, those metal detectors don't work. I have one that won't find anything!" Ever hear that? I sincerely believe that cheap detectors have done more harm to our hobby than just about anything else.

Search for Value

When seeking that *right* detector one of your major considerations must always be value. Of course, value is the relationship between what an item costs and how well it performs. High quality detectors may seem expensive, but you'll never "lose your money" by purchasing one of them because you'll always have a high quality detector. On the other hand, if you buy a cheap, off-brand model, you'll essentially lose *all* your money because your so-called detector won't detect or do any of the things you expect. You're left with nothing!

You can see that I'm evading the question I posed about price. And, it's a difficult one...somewhat like asking, "How much should a car cost?"

My company makes a wide range of detectors, and we sell lots of each model. Yet one of our continuing goals is to give every customer the most *value* for his or her money. Right now, our basic "starter" detector has a suggested retail price of just over $200; and, depending on your dealer, you may beat this price. Let me urge you, however, not to buy a model from any manufacturer that has a list price of much less than $200. Many of you will probably want to pay more to get some of the features we're going to discuss.

For example, you probably won't be able to buy a quality one-touch detector for this low price. But, the ease of operation you'll enjoy with this type of instrument and the greater amount of treasure you'll find with it are well worth the extra dollars.

And, you may be pleasantly surprised at how little more a Garrett OneTouch detector will cost.

Still, when folks our age talk about "hundreds" of dollars, they're usually talking about what sounds like a lot of money — it does to me — but, remember, a quality metal detector will literally last a lifetime. The first one I ever made is now in our Garrett Museum, but I could take it into the park today and find coins. I'm continually amazed at how well our detectors endure the treatment they receive. And, I guarantee that if you select metal detecting as a hobby, you won't ever be forced to buy bait, lures and balls or to pay greens fees or country club dues like you would with some other, more expensive, pastimes.

A popular adjective for detectors today seems to be "simple." A competitor describes his instrument as "the ultimate in simplicity." Believe me, it isn't. Don't let yourself be taken in by advertising claims. Make certain that the detector you buy is ready to hunt when you turn it on. You don't want to have to set several controls or — perish the thought — load a program. I don't know about you, but having to *load* a program into my detector or to remember numerical codes to understand its signals ranks right up there with programming the VCR in simplicity. What you see is what you get with a Garrett OneTouch detector, and that's the way I like it!

Read this book carefully to learn about detectors. You can also study the various magazines and other books about detectors. Notice which models that other hobbyists are using.

Select an instrument built by a progressive company with a history of engineering excellence...a company that has steadily introduced quality improvements. Does the manufacturer test his own instruments? Does he get out into the field and use them under all kinds of situations? Does he travel to various locations to test varying soil conditions to insure his detectors work regardless of conditions? Are company engineers active in the field?

I am confident that more than two thirds of the men, women and children who use metal detectors hunt essentially just for lost coins. Now, that doesn't mean they'll pass up any jewelry they find (or an outlaw's cache of holdup loot, for that matter)! But, the goal of most individuals is to enjoy a hobby that can help pay for itself — and, to make it pay by finding coins. In fact, I believe that more than half of the instruments our company sells are never used for anything but coin hunting.

For this reason, *every* Garrett detector is designed to find coins. Perhaps that statement is true of other manufacturers. But, the point I'm making is that you should get a *general purpose* detector and not some "specialized" model...unless you're pretty sure of yourself and what you want to accomplish with a detector.

Because it would be presumptuous of me to discuss products of other manufacturers, I talk only about Garrett detectors. Speaking of them, however, I will say that each of our GTA series of instruments is well suited to any type of treasure hunting and automatic operation and simplicity of operation make each of them excellent for the beginning hobbyist. I offer an unqualified recommendation of any Garrett GTA detector as an excellent all-purpose instrument.

Nevertheless, there can be no argument that a number of detectors are available today in all price ranges that will perform admirably in many situations and under extreme environmental conditions; and, a few detectors will do most jobs quite satisfactorily.

Speaking of detectors...and their controls: make certain just how many there are on the model you select. Will "one touch" really make this detector ready to hunt? You go into the field to have fun by finding treasure, not to prove your expertise by manipulating controls on an electronic instrument. What does each control do? Are all absolutely necessary? Are they smooth to operate?

When you put the detector through its paces over various targets, does it respond smoothly or are there sudden changes and squawks and squeals in the audio over and above the "blip-like" sounds normally produced by certain trash targets?

Quality construction should be demanded! If you suspect less-than-the-best construction in any single one of a detector's components, it may pay you to double-check everything else associated with this particular instrument.

Please don't rely too much on the results of so-called "air tests'" i.e., checking out the distance that a detector will detect various small and large targets with nothing but air between the searchcoil and target. Of course, you'll probably want to determine a detector's sensitivity for yourself in such a test. If so, try to measure detection distance with a small coin like a penny. Don't use a silver dollar! The smaller coin is a better test target. If a detector will pick up a penny to a good distance, it will surely detect a silver dollar to an even greater one.

Let me point out, however, that the new computerized detectors have made "air tests" completely invalid.

Remember that microprocessor-controlled circuitry enables a detector to analyze simultaneously all soil conditions over which it is searching, as well as the target(s) beneath its searchcoil. Thus, computerized detectors with microprocessor controls, when properly designed, can sometimes detect objects at greater distances (depths) in the ground than in the air!

It's a fact.

Selection Checkpoints

When selecting a metal detector, here are a few specific points to consider:

– The equipment should be lightweight and engineered for comfortable use over extended periods of time. Remember, however, that the lightest equipment may not be sufficiently durable.

– The equipment should have only the controls — one-touch, preferably — and functions necessary to do the job you want it to do.

– Unnecessary controls and functions complicate the instrument's operation and will make it harder to use.

– Extra controls and functions can also confuse an operator, especially one who uses the equipment just occasionally. Improper adjustment, even if only a temporary condition, can decrease the effectiveness of a search...and make a hunt less enjoyable.

– These controls and functions are the minimum that should be accepted:

1. Circuitry that automatically eliminates (ground balances) the effects of iron minerals in the soil and/or ocean salt, if you are a beachcomber.

2. Some easy means of eliminating unwanted targets, combined, if possible, with an effective means for identifying targets.

3. Headphone jack for this essential accessory.

4. Compatibility with different sizes and types of coils. As you gain expertise, you may want to experiment with different sizes. Make certain your detector will accept these other sizes and types...and that they are available!

5. Circuit or means to check the batteries.

6. Access to batteries (if not rechargeable) should be easy. Are the required batteries readily available and reasonably priced?

Evaluation Summation

When evaluating a specific detector, here is a summary of things to look for...questions you *should* ask...

• Is the detector easy to operate? How much "adjustment" is *really* necessary? In other words, is it really a one-touch detector?

• Is it truly a computerized instrument with microprocessor controls?

• Is the equipment designed so that weight is always properly balanced?

• Is the detector too heavy? Now, it may feel just fine the first time you pick it up, but decide how it will feel after you swing it for several hours. Believe me, when you're on the track of treasure, the hours fly by. And, you will not be satisfied with a detector whose weight has cramped up your muscles to such an extent that you are forced to stop hunting today and may not be able to get out tomorrow.

• Are the instrument and its components well protected for storage, transportation and use?

• Is the detector easily assembled and are the batteries and all controls readily accessible and properly located?

• Is the equipment constructed with strength and durability? Look for areas that are mechanically weak and flex easily. Look for controls, meters or other items that protrude and which could be broken off. Are there sufficient fastening devices, locking nuts, etc., to keep the handle and stems from working loose?

• Is plastic used properly in the equipment? Are the searchcoils made of heavy gauge ABS for long wear and abrasion resistance? Is the plastic stem or stem extension made of strong materials that will not be expected to crack or break?

• Are desired operational features such as a battery check, detection depth (sensitivity) control, discrimination, ground balance and earphone jack included?

• Are desired accessory searchcoils available? Can all searchcoils be submerged? You may want to search in a shallow stream.

• Are controls clearly marked? Is the instruction manual adequate, yet easy to understand? It will pay you to take a close look at the manual and see how fully it describes the detector.

• Is video instruction available? It is also good here to take a look at the video itself to see just how clearly it explains detector operation.

• Is the equipment designed to do the jobs intended? Is it suitable for the operating environments in which it will be used?

Choosing the *right* detector for you can be a major factor in your enjoyment and appreciation of treasure hunting. If you're not happy with the instrument you're using, you're not going to get all the pleasure possible out of this great hobby.

And, what a tragedy that would be!

For this reason I implore you to select carefully. Be as honest as you can about how you will use your detector and then select one that is just right for you!

Become a Dealer

Before closing this chapter that discusses economics, I'd like to report how a few of our older customers have combined their enjoyment of a new hobby with their business experience by becoming Garrett dealers. They certainly didn't want to "go back to work," but sought simply to reduce their costs in the hobby. Yet, as it has turned out, some of them have earned considerable profits.

Now, I'm not talking about opening a shop and incurring the expense and trouble of running a business enterprise. My goodness, you retired to get away from that! No, these individuals I'm talking about simply responded to queries from and interest shown by their friends. As successful users of metal detectors, they wanted to help spread the hobby and cut their costs at the same time.

One of these is a gentlemen who spends a great deal of time traveling around the country in an RV. He took up metal detecting to have something to do after he arrives at his various locations. And, he became quite good at finding treasure with his detector. When his RV companions expressed interest, he began helping them buy detectors. He continues to be truly amazed at the success of his new "business."

I can't speak for other manufacturers, but I know that Garrett welcomes inquiries from anyone who is sincerely interested in selling our products.

We also enjoy talking to individuals who are simply interested in learning more about metal detecting. To help each customer select a detector that is "best" for that particular individual, Garrett produces a *Buyer's Guide* which includes complete information about all of our detectors as well as much other information pertaining to treasure hunting with a metal detector.

Charles Garrett

This *Guide* is updated annually and will be sent free to anyone writing Garrett at 1881 W. State Street, Garland, TX 75042, or calling our toll-free number, 800-527-4011.

We also produce a publication, *The Garrett Searcher*, which contains stories of metal detector successes as well as "how-to" articles and special offers on Garrett products and Ram books. We urge you to let us add you to this mailing list. Just write the above address or call the toll-free number. And, when you find that first gold coin, we may want to include your picture in the next issue!

Let us hear from you!

Using a Detector

t's especially easy if you're using today's *one-touch* computerized instrument! Of course, this chapter will explain clearly how you can find treasure with any good detector. Always remember that well designed detectors are not complicated or difficult to learn to use.

This chapter is for all metal detector operators...but, primarily those relatively new to the hobby. It contains practical methods, tips and procedures recommended to every treasure hunter. Learn these simple techniques, and you can enjoy the hobby by spending as little or as much time as you wish. The choice is yours!

Still, the amount of success you ultimately obtain with any kind of metal detector (or with any other hobby) will be in direct proportion to the amount of time and study that you devote it. For those just starting out in the hobby, I urge you to select a computerized one-touch detector...even if it costs a little more. You'll be glad you did when you find yourself discovering treasures that others have passed over! And, you will be more successful with the hobby of metal detecting. No matter how good some of the older detectors were (and still are) they can't match the depth and sensitivity of the new computerized instruments.

It's important to remember that detectors being sold today vary widely in quality. Some will barely detect a coin one inch deep, while computerized instruments will let you detect that same coin at extreme depths in the same soil and even indicate its denomination. So, if you are determined to use an older detector, make certain that it is a high quality instrument from a respected manufacturer. Then you should learn how to use it well by following instructions found in your owner's manual and this and other books.

With any detector, however, the first instruction is the same: *Read your instruction manual!* Carefully study the operator's manual that accompanied your detector. At our Company we recommend that you examine this manual *before* you purchase a detector. If the manufacturer has "skimped" on providing instructions and advice, you might find yourself shorted in other areas of an instrument.

On the other hand, an extremely detailed manual that you find hard to understand could well indicate a detector that's going to prove just as complicated...one that will be difficult to learn how to use. New one-touch computerized and microprocessor-controlled detectors are *simple to use*, not difficult.

Getting Started

When you begin your home study, please don't make the mistake of immediately assembling the detector and running outside to begin looking for treasure. Actually, I suggest that you pay no attention to your new detector at first, but simply read its instruction manual. Read it several times. The first time through, read it from front to back without stopping. If a video instruction tape is available for your detector, watch it carefully. Then, assemble your instrument according to the instructions on the tape and in the manual. Take time to do it right.

With a one-touch detector you're now ready to hunt for treasure. And, that's what you should do!

Modern detectors have many capabilities beyond those that are available with a single touch. But, it's the simple touch of a single control that let's you find treasure with a modern detector, so let's go find some.

Start out with the typical general purpose searchcoil which is eight or nine inches in diameter. Turn the detector on with a single touch, and you're ready to hunt. No need to wave the searchcoil up and down. Simply lower it to a height of about two inches above the ground and begin scanning.

Scanning speed is very important. Your detector will operate and analyze targets over a wide range of scanning speeds even though ultra-fast or very slow techniques can limit success. We recommend that you operate at a speed of between one to two feet per second. Go even slower, and you might be surprised at your increased success, especially in areas with lots of junk targets. We suggest that you try a test. Slow down and scan with your searchcoil very deliberately. You may reap great benefits.

Some of you may prefer to scan with a searchcoil lightly skimming the ground. This is fine; don't worry about it. Our only recommendation about such activity is that you use the appropriate skid plate (coil cover) to protect your searchcoil against unnecessary abrasion and wear.

Improved deepseeking circuitry of modern instruments requires that you keep the searchcoil moving slightly for detection to occur. This is not difficult, and you'll soon become used to the fact that your detection sound ceases when you hold the coil still.

Don't get in a hurry, and don't try to cover an acre in 10 minutes. Always remember that what you are looking for is probably buried just below the sweep you are now making with your searchcoil. It's not across the field.

When the sound increases and/or an indication is shown on the LCD panel or meter, a target is buried in the ground below the searchcoil.

When a searchcoil is being scanned over the ground or in the water, a detector reports information on targets...

– Through increases or decreases in audible volume (universal on all detectors);

– Graphic information presented on LCD meters or

– Meter deflections.

Remember that acceptable objects cause the audio or visual indicators to increase in amplitude. LCDs and meter indicators can provide additional information concerning the possible "value" of targets. Some of the new LCD's even indicate just what you've discovered.

Don't worry — at least at first — about what you are finding. As you recover various targets, you will find yourself getting better and better with your detector. You will become more at ease in using it, and the quantity of found items will be growing at an accelerated rate.

Techniques of scanning for treasure with a metal detector are many and varied. Here are some simple recommendations:

• Keep the searchcoil level as you scan and always scan slowly and methodically; scan the searchcoil from side to side and in a straight line in front of you.

• Do not scan the searchcoil in an arc unless the arc width is narrow (about two feet) or unless you are scanning extremely slowly. The straight-line scan method allows you to cover more ground width in each sweep and permits you to keep the searchcoil level throughout each sweep. This method reduces skipping and helps you overlap more uniformly.

• Overlap by advancing the searchcoil as much as 50% of the coil's diameter at the end of each sweep path. Occasionally scan an area from a different angle. Do not raise the searchcoil above scanning level at the end of each sweep. When the searchcoil begins to reach the extremes of each sweep, you will find yourself rotating your upper body to stretch out for an even wider sweep. This gives the double benefit of scanning a wider sweep and gaining additional exercise.

• "Pinpointing" is the hobby's term for precisely locating your target before you dig. Most of the more expensive detectors offer what is called "automatic pinpointing," a special control that lets you hover your searchcoil and zero-in on the target. Slowly making a simple "X" with the coil over a target will generally serve the same purpose. Manual pinpointing is not hard; it just may take a little practice.

• You can learn to use a probe to locate the exact spot where coins are buried; this will help you retrieve coins with minimum damage to grass and the target.

• How do you dig a target? Progressive detector manufacturers will offer you probes, digging tools and sand scoops to aid you in recovery. But, I suggest you use your imagination and one or more of those tools you've probably accumulated in a lifetime of gardening and/or yard work.

• Always remember, however, to make as small a hole as possible and to fill in your hole after you dig a target. Holes are not only unsightly, but they can be dangerous to people walking in the area. Perhaps it might be you! Before filling a hole, however, be sure to check it again with your detector to make certain you have recovered everything in and around it. It's embarrassing to have someone recover a target in the loose dirt of a hole you originally dug and filled. I know; it's happened to me!

• Run-down batteries are by far the single most common source of detector "failure;" be sure to check your batteries before venturing out, and carry spare batteries whenever you are searching.

During the learning phase with your own detector, keep in mind that you should work smarter, not harder.

As you begin to understand your detector, this little "game" may aid in your enjoyment of the hobby. Each time you receive a signal — before you dig — try to guess what the target is, what size it is, its shape and its depth. Analyze the audio and/or meter signals. Say to yourself, "This is a coin," or "This is a bottlecap. It is about three inches deep." Then pay careful attention when you dig the object. Try to determine exactly how deep it is and how it was lying in the ground.

Did you guess right? Great! If not, try to determine why. The more you follow this practice, the greater your success will be. You will quickly learn how to use and actually "read" your instrument so that you can understand everything it is telling you.

Remember that a quality detector will never "lie" to you. It will simply report what is beneath its searchcoil. It's up to you to interpret this information.

Increasing Your Enjoyment

Now, what I've just outlined is really *all* you need to know about getting started correctly. Follow these instructions with a modern instrument, and you will have success that will enable you to enjoy your hobby and take pleasure in what you have found.

After you've become comfortable with your detector and learned how easy it is to find treasure with it, however, you may want to learn more about this instrument and its capabilities. Although you really never have to do more than press a single control to find treasure with the new one-touch detectors, you'll probably want to become familiar with all of your instrument's functions. You'll want to learn exactly what it will do for you.

So, it's back to the Owner's Manual. You can skip the parts that concern assembly and searching, but read the rest of it carefully. If you detector permits regulating the sound threshold, you'll want to learn how to do it. Follow instructions carefully to set a minimum threshold level. If silent operation is desired, always make certain that such operation is just below an audible level. Many of us never use silent audio since it is possible to overlook "fringe" signals and miss targets.

The instruction manual and video should guide you through all of these adjustments which you can make through the bench-testing process. Lay your detector on a wooden

Walking in a straight line, Ed Morris, a retiree in Santa Maria, CA, is swinging his searchcoil carefully and deliberately to scan this sandy playground area.

bench or table. Do not use a table with metal legs and braces because the metal could interfere with your testing. Begin with the part of your instruction manual that describes detection of metal. Go through the procedure! If your detector is equipped with a sensitivity or detection depth control, test the detector at several levels. Test the instrument with various metal targets. Make the adjustments discussed in the manual or video that let you accomplish different objectives with the detector. Try as many of these variations with different targets on the bench as possible.

Discrimination

This is a popular word with detector hobbyists that can be defined simply as the elimination of unwanted targets. Modern one-touch detectors have simple discrimination pre-set at the factory to keep you from finding most bottlecaps and similar metallic trash.

After you have used your detector for several hours, you can begin to test its discrimination capabilities for yourself. Read about this in your owner's manual. But, whatever you do, don't use too much discrimination...just enough to eliminate from detection the junk you may have been digging.

Pulltabs are a story in themselves. Simply stated, they cause trouble. And, they're hard to discriminate out because such discrimination can also eliminate nickels and some gold rings. I suggest that you try to set your detector's discrimination to eliminate pulltabs only when you feel such discrimination is absolutely necessary.

If you haven't started using headphones, now's the time to learn how important they are. Headphones will permit you to

Because recovering your finds is such an important part of the metal detecting hobby, good techniques such as Ed is using here must be developed.

dig coins that you couldn't detect just by listening to a detector's speaker. You'll hear sounds you didn't hear before

After you have even more experience and are beginning to get comfortable with your detector, it's time to go back over the same areas you searched before you learned how to use your machine. You'll be surprised at the quantity of coins and other objects you missed. In fact, each time you come back to these places you'll find more coins and other treasures, especially at greater depths.

When you begin using controls other than the "one-touch," remember to keep the Detection Depth (sensitivity) control at about 75%. Rarely will you find interference at this level. Whenever you begin hearing erratic sounds, it's often because sensitivity is set too high. Before you blame your detector or the soil's high mineral content, turn down your depth setting. The lower setting will also let you work in more areas.

Scan with the searchcoil about two inches above the ground and scan at a moderate speed. Even in areas with large amounts of "junk" metal, which make scanning very difficult, reduced detection depth and moderate scanning speed let you hear individual target signals rather than just a jumbled mass of sounds.

Success stories are written every day. A lot of treasure is being found and a lot of treasure is waiting to be found where you live. Detectors are not magic wands, but when used correctly they will locate buried and concealed treasure. Use a high quality detector and keep your faith in it. Have patience and continue using your instrument until you have it mastered. Success will be yours!

Make Your Own Test Plot

One of the first things many new detector owners do is to bury a few coins to see how deeply they can be detected. The usual result...*disappointment.* You see, newly buried coins are usually quite difficult to detect. The longer an object has been buried, the easier it can be detected. Not only is a coin is first buried, but no "halo effect" has been developed. As time passes, coins become more closely associated, electrically, with surrounding earth materials and the molecules of metal begin to leave and move out into the surrounding soil. Also, it is theorized that in some cases (especially in salt water) the coin's surface becomes a better conductor. In certain areas it is believed that coins buried for some time can be detected at more than twice the depth of coins that have just been buried.

After your interest in the hobby grows, you might want to construct your own test plot to help you learn the capabilities of your detector. First of all, select the area for it and scan the area thoroughly with no discrimination so that you can remove all metal from the ground. Select targets such as various coins, a bottlecap, a nail and a pulltab. Select also a pint jar filled with scrap copper and/or aluminum metal, a long object such as a foot-long pipe and a large object such as a gallon can. Bury all these objects in rows about three feet apart and make a map showing where each item is buried. Be sure to note its depth.

Bury pennies at varying depths, beginning at one inch. Continue, with the deepest buried about six inches deep. Bury one at about two inches but stand it on edge. Bury a penny at about two inches with a bottlecap about four inches off to one side. Bury the bottlecap, nail and pulltab separately about two inches deep. Bury the jar at ten inches to the top of its lid. Bury the pipe horizontally three or four inches deep. Bury the gallon can with the lid 18 inches below the surface.

The purpose of the buried coins is to familiarize you with the sound of money. If you can't detect the deeper coins, don't worry. After a while, you'll be able to detect them quickly. If you can detect everything in your test plot, rebury some items deeper. The penny buried next to the bottle cap can give you experience in "super sniping" with a smaller searchcoil and will help you learn to distinguish individual objects. The jar and gallon can will help you learn to recognize "dull" sounds of large, deeply buried objects. The pipe will help you learn to contour. Check the targets with and without headphones. You'll be amazed at the difference headphones make.

I also suggest that you vary the Depth (sensitivity) control to help you recognize the sounds that your detector will make at various "depths." This will clearly reveal how "fringe-area" responses sound.

From time to time you may want to expand your test plot, rebury the targets deeper or experiment with new ones. Always leave an area totally void of targets. You will want to bury new ones from time to time to see how they sound or simply to test out your detection ideas.

Your test plot can be important because your success in scanning over it will be a measure of how well you are progressing and how well you have learned your equipment. Remember to make an accurate map and keep it up to date when you change and/or add to your test plot.

Miscellaneous Tips

When searching areas adjacent to wire fences, metal buildings, metal parking meter posts, etc., reduce detection depth and scan the searchcoil parallel to the structure. This lets you get as close to it as possible.

Coins lying in the ground at an angle may be missed on one searchcoil pass but detected when the searchcoil approaches from a different angle.

If your detector has a volume control, keep it set at maximum. Don't confuse volume with audio (threshold) control. You should use earphones that have individual earphone volume adjustment and set each one to suit yourself.

Use your common sense. *Think* your way through perplexing situations. Remember, expertise is gained through research, patience, enthusiasm and the use of common sense.

Don't expect to find tons of treasure every time you go out! In fact, there may be times when you don't find anything. But the hobby's real joy and the reward of detecting is never knowing what you'll dig up next!

Where to Hunt

My life has been spent developing search and recovery skills that others did not know or were not willing to take the necessary time to learn. And, one of the most valuable of these is knowing *where* to hunt. You can be using the finest metal detector that I or anyone else manufactures, but if there's no treasure to be found where you're scanning, you'll go home with little in your pouch.

A successful hobbyist must have many strings in his bow. He (or, she) must have the proper attitude...the desire and the curiosity, if you will. The successful treasure hunter must not be afraid of hard work. A good metal detector is a must, along with the knowledge of how to use it. The instrument alone is never enough. I've said many times that I can find more treasure with my first Garrett BFO Hunter detector than another treasure hunter who's using a more modern instrument, but one with which he is unfamiliar.

And, finally, the successful hobbyist must hunt in the right place. Where is this *right* place? Well, that's what this chapter is all about.

There appears to be a misconception today among some who are associated with our hobby. I hear an increasing number cry that the "good" places to hunt are disappearing...that adverse rules and regulations are making it impossible for us to find treasure. And, I hear others who moan that it's so much harder to find treasure now than it was 10 or 20 years ago.

Now, both of these statements are absolutely correct! Rules and regulations governing (yes, limiting) the use of metal detectors are becoming more prevalent. And, I'll certainly testify that it's not as easy to find treasure today as it was when I began metal detecting 30 years go. I should know because many of those old coins and relics that I dug up an inch or two deep seemed to have been just waiting for my instrument to find them.

Most of the easy finds may be gone! And, that's all there is to that.

But, the misconception that concerns me is the one that says *there's just no place left to hunt!*

Wrong, wrong, wrong!

Potential hunting sites are still virtually limitless. Finding a good one now simply requires more imagination and more research that it once did...which merely makes the hobby more interesting. And, it should also be more profitable! Good research will lead us to better sites, and new OneTouch computerized instruments will recover those old and deeply buried coins that might have been left behind by hobbyists with older or inferior detectors.

Still, you'll probably have to hunt just a little smarter to recover treasures like we were finding 10 or 15 years ago. But, these treasures are there. I'm finding them by hunting smarter, and I hear from countless others who are having similar success.

I believe that finding some kind of treasure will always be an easy matter for someone who knows how to use a good metal detector. But, it's up to you to perfect your skills and techniques if you decide that you really want to pursue and become successful at this fascinating hobby of treasure hunting...a hobby that can not only pay for itself but can prove *very* rewarding.

This is true whether your goal be a "grand treasure," one you must spend considerable time researching and recovering, or whether you just want become proficient at a hobby that will let you enjoy yourself while finding pocket change in the park or on a beach.

The first rule of treasure hunting, I believe, is to hunt in your own back yard...sometimes, literally. Hobbyists, especially beginners, should not be seeking treasure buried far away...in another city...another state...another land, but treasure buried literally within a stone's throw away from them.

The mistake too many individuals make when they set out to hunt is ignoring nearby treasures while they speed off in search of Captain Kidd's buried chest or that fabled Wells Fargo box hidden by Butch and Sundance.

Successful hobbyists have learned that there are dozens of "little treasures" concealed in practically every accessible yard or park of any city or town — valuables that were lost just this morning or long ago...yet, all lost and forgotten, but nevertheless well worth finding. It may be more than just a little treasure. It may be a hermit's cache of gold coins...a farmer's "post-hole bank," his wife's "butter-and-egg" money buried in the garden. These are the treasures that I urge all hobbyists to learn to find.

Does it now take an "expert" to locate this lost wealth? No. Treasures are still being found by practically anyone...young or old, male or female, retired persons searching almost full time or the weekend vacationer. I am confident that success will always come in direct proportion to effort expended...and, sometimes the effort will be little more than walking down a beautiful and sunny beach.

Countless millions of coins have been lost and await recovery by the metal detector hobbyist. Don't make the mistake of believing there are no coins to be found where you live. If you don't have the experience now, you soon will gain the knowledge to convince yourself that coins are truly found everywhere. The first place every person should start searching is right in his own backyard before branching out from there. Many people erroneously believe there is nothing in their areas worth searching for. The truth is *all* the good coin hunting sites will *never* be cleaned out.

Charles Garrett

Exploring a ghost town is a popular and rewarding hobby which includes a number of activities. In ghost towns you may discover old coins, perhaps a buried treasure cache, relics or antiques dating back to the earliest settlers...or lost items from only yesterday. Any place people have gathered will produce relics and coins. There are thousands of abandoned town sites, old forts, homesteads and farmhouse locations. The list is endless. Finding a place to search should never be your problem! Finding the time needed to pursue and enjoy the hobby is often more of a challenge. A quality metal detector is a must for such hunting since most surface items have already been picked up, and those remaining will be buried — perhaps, deeply.

Cache hunting is seeking money or valuables that have been put away or cached by someone... the little old lady's "hard times" coins she buried in a fruit jar in her garden 50 or 100 years ago, the old hermit's "bank" he kept hidden in the bottom of a fence post hole or, that fabled washtub filled with gold coins. These are all caches. Thousands of such treasures exist, and many will be surprisingly easy to find with a metal detector. They are literally waiting for the diligent hobbyist who uses the techniques of proper research to seek them out. Buried only a few inches deep or at arm's length below ground surface, they will stay under the earth forever if they are not dug up by the treasure hunter. Caches can be found anywhere...in an old chicken coop, halfway between the well and a tree, between two trees, in the ground, under the horse stall, in the walls of houses and barns, etc.

Collecting and studying battlefield relics constitutes an interesting pastime for many people. Of course, the great war in this country was the Civil War, and values placed on artifacts and other items from this time are often astronomical. The finding of battlefield relics brings history so close that one can visualize it in the making.

The numerous battle and skirmish sites of the eastern and western campaigns and naval operations abound in relics and artifacts valued by war buffs and professional collectors. All types of weapons or instruments of the war are being located by persistent metal detector enthusiasts. Many of the better known battle areas in the country, however, are protected by state and federal governments. These areas are strictly "off limits" to all metal detector operators. This is a fact of life that we must accept because there's little chance that it will ever change!

Yet such restrictions need not limit successful relic hunting. I personally know many individuals who remain quite active in locating numerous Civil War sites to search successfully without ever thinking about hunting in restricted areas. They are proving that the treasures are there; it's up to us to seek them out through proper research. Just the other day a friend told me of a Tennessee "skirmish" site that he had found. This site, previously unknown to relic hunters, yielded fired as well as dropped projectiles and other items.

And, how about beaches? Sure, some of them are closed to metal detection, but plenty of others are still available. On some beaches there are roped-off areas designed for swimming. Search these places first! Strike up a conversation with the lifeguard or concession stand operators. It may be that the swimming areas of bygone days were located elsewhere on the beach. You would certainly want to search those sites. Also, lifeguards may know where rings and valuables are reported to have been lost. Try working along the water's edge at both low and high tides; both could be profitable. You will encounter much less trash near the water, but remember, some very valuable coins and jewelry have been found back away from the beach in the heavy traffic areas. There are thousands of swimming beaches no longer used. Visit your library and do a little research to locate these older resort and health spa swimming areas where much treasure awaits discovery.

It's true that each state has its own laws concerning where you can hunt for treasure and whether you may keep treasure when it is found, and there are local ordinances as well. There is certainly no need to grow bitter about them! You should become familiar with these laws, just as you are aware of other laws that govern your daily activities. This is more important now than ever before because penalties are sometimes severe. And, remember the old truism: *Ignorance of the law is no excuse.*

All states have laws against trespassing. If a sign says, "Keep Out," do just that. It is always best to seek permission. With the proper attitude and a true explanation of your purpose, you will be surprised at the cooperation you will receive from most landowners. The majority of them will be curious enough about your metal detector and what you hope to find, to agree to let you search. Offer to split, giving them 25% (or less) of all you find and they will usually be more willing.

On the other hand, when an individual tells you to stop searching and orders you off the property...well, you leave! I can only think of one instance in which I disobeyed a person who ordered me to stop searching and leave. But, I had the permission of the property owner to hunt there, and I made certain that the person who had ordered me to leave did not realize that I was continuing to search. You know, I can't even recall what treasure I was seeking or even if I found it, but it must have been important at the time.

You will be pleasantly surprised at how much public property is open for you to search with a metal detector to your heart's content. Yet these public areas will not remain open if we hobbyists do not behave properly as we search for treasure on there. Do not damage the grass or shrubbery or leave behind trash or holes. Many park superintendents have learned that because conscientious coin hunters pick up trash, the grounds will be in better shape than before the hobbyists came. I urge each of you to help prove that such a belief is true. There are several ways to remove coins from the ground properly, and you can develop your own techniques. All treasure hunters must become aware of their responsibility to protect the property of others and to keep public property fit for all. Persons who destroy property, dig large holes and leave them unfilled, or tear down buildings in search of valuables, should not to be called treasure hunters — but, more properly, looters and scavengers.

And, this brings up a situation that is quite painful to many of us who truly love the hobby of metal detecting. Unscrupulous treasure hunters are literally ruining this wonderful hobby for the rest of us. Ed Morris, a long-time California detectorist, is a good friend of mine. He tells of a fairground where he has made many excellent finds over the years. Yet, this fairground is now "off limits" to his metal detector because of the damage inflicted on the property by other treasure hunters. Sure, Ed was conscientious, but he's still barred from hunting in this good location because of the rude and selfish behavior of others.

I urge every hobbyist to leave every site where you hunt in better physical condition than you found it!

There are approximately 350 treasure hunting clubs in the United States with a total of over 500 clubs located throughout the world. Why not join one and take an active part? Clubs are an invaluable source of information. You can learn about metal detectors and treasure hunting locations from those who are active in the field in that particular area. You will meet people, share their success stories, and perhaps gain a few hunting partners. You will be encouraged by found treasure, and you can perhaps swap some of your treasure and build up your collection.

The hobby and sport of metal detecting has been kept clean and dignified by people who care... people who are responsible for the consequences of their actions and are concerned with the rights of others. Most detector owners go out of their way to protect this most rewarding and enjoyable hobby and to share their enjoyment with others. Keeping the hobby clean takes the constant effort and dedication of everyone...not just a few. So, as you go about enjoying your leisure — or perhaps full-time — activity, be professional! Be worthy of this fine hobby!

Chapter 7 — Heart of the Hobby...

Coin Hunting

When most people think of hunting with a metal detector, they think of searching for coins that have just been lost by children on a playground or on a beach. To an extent they are right, for such hunting can be quick, easy and *profitable*. And, it's the type of hunting that can take place anytime with as many or as few hours spent as the hobbyist desires. Plus, with a one-touch detector it can be accomplished successfully with very little practice.

But..."Pennies?" you may ask. How can it ever be "profitable" to search for pennies?

Who's talking about pennies? I said *coins,* and it doesn't matter who lost them — or when!

Hunting for coins is the heart and soul of the metal detecting hobby because literally everybody hunts for coins. They are certainly the initial target sought by most first-time detector owners of any age. And, why do so many people hunt for coins?

Because...they are *there!*

Think of all the coins that you have handled in your life...thousands and thousands. And, your experiences were shared by most other folks. So, where are the millions of coins that you and other individuals handled?

These coins were made of metal. Not many of them were used enough to "wear out."

Would you believe that the number of *lost* coins far exceeds the total in circulation today? Then, just think about all of the lost coins — now lying on or beneath the ground, hidden in houses and buildings or in waters of lakes, streams and oceans. Coins just awaiting discovery — "finders keepers" coins that belong to the first person to find them or dig them up — exceed in number and *far surpass in value* all the coins currently in commerce, savings and collections.

Lost coins can be found all over the world. Except perhaps for the polar icecaps and barren Asian peaks, I sincerely believe there is no place on the face of the earth where coins cannot be found with a metal detector...and, in abundance if the site has never before been searched. Literally multitudes of coins can be found everywhere. You just have to look for them. Why am I so sure about this? I've proved it for myself!

Coin-hunting is the usual introduction to the fascinating and rewarding hobby of searching with a metal detector. Let me warn you, however, that you'll soon find yourself "hooked." After you begin finding coins — and especially when you make that first "big" find — coin-hunting will be ever on your mind. No matter where you are or what you are doing, you'll find yourself subconsciously evaluating the coin-hunting prospects of that location.

And, you know what? *You'll love it!*

If you are totally new to the hobby of metal detecting, you may already be questioning your competence as a coin hunter. And, honestly, aren't you a little suspicious that all you'll get from this hobby is exercise and fresh air — which you probably need more of, anyway. But, read on, and you'll learn how easy it is to find coins with a modern metal detector.

I believe that every instrument I've ever designed and built was used at one time or another to search for coins. I'm also confident that many of these detectors were and are still being used for no other purpose. Oh, jewelry and other valuable items are certainly sought, but coins are the thrust of the search for most hobbyists, no matter what their intentions.

So, all detector hobbyists should master coin-hunting techniques which will be used in all other forms of THing.

The recommended detector for hunting coins is a modern instrument with automatic ground balancing and good discrimination. The best instruments, however, are the new computerized detectors with microprocessor controls that provide alternatives between several modes and discrimination levels. Of course, any detector with an All Metal mode will find more and deeper coins, but in the All Metal mode every target should be dug.

Coin hunting is a field in which you can especially excel with one of the Ultra GTA detectors, the Grand Master Hunter CX II or III or the Master Hunter CX...Garrett's computerized detectors with microprocessor controls! Any of these versatile instruments will be found especially suitable for coin hunting.

In fact, the Ultra GTA detectors were designed primarily as coin hunters. The precise target identification possible with microprocessor-controlled circuitry permits detection at extreme depths. Combine this with the GTA's light weight and ease of handling and you have a superb instrument for finding coins.

Whenever you turn a GTA detector on, it's automatically ready to hunt for coins...whether you're in a park or on a beach or wherever.

Discrimination pre-set at the factory will respond ideally to conditions normally encountered. This discrimination is designed to eliminate detection of lower conductivity trash targets normally encountered in coin hunting, such as bottlecaps and most pulltabs.

Coins & Junk

There will be times when you hear a good solid detection tone while scanning over a spot in one direction and just an audio "blip" when scanning from another angle. Although this is most likely a junk target, we advise you not just to walk away from it. Continue scanning back and forth across it from numerous angles. Draw your imaginary "X;" slide your searchcoil from side to side. Even push the coil forward and backward. Listen to the sound carefully. If you ever get the coin tone in both directions (headphones are a real help here), dig the target. You'll probably find a coin in close proximity to some sort of junk.

We know how much will power it takes to resist these blips coming over your headphones or from the audio speaker beneath the armrest of your GTA. You know a target exists, and it's human nature to want to dig them all! Remember, however, that a quality modern detector will never lie to you. Its LCD display and audible sounds will generally identify all objects being detected beneath the searchcoil at any given instant. Of course, because adjacent trash can sometimes "confuse" the detector, you may want to dig all targets. That's what I often do...especially when there's a lot of trash!

I recommend that coin hunters begin with the standard 8- or 9-inch general purpose searchcoil for scanning most parks, playgrounds, beaches and other conventional coin hunting areas. It is the best all-around searchcoil. Numerous letters and personal inquiries regularly ask about the occasional use of larger coils. My answer is a definite *yes*...because larger coils can detect deeper, yet find even the smallest coins.

Now, those of you to whom this is a new idea may be asking just when to use the larger searchcoil. Good question!

After you scan an area with the 8 1/2-inch coil, you may suspect that you are encountering deep targets that give you only a faint signal, even with headphones. If so, you're detecting at the outer limits of that all-purpose searchcoil, and you may be missing deeper coins. You need the additional detection depth that is available with the 12 1/2-inch searchcoil. After scanning such an area thoroughly with your 8 1/2-inch searchcoil, go back over it again with a larger coil,

To find old coins hobbyists must seek them in places where they could have been lost many years ago as Lewis Ernest has done in his quest for treasure.

scanning very slowly and using headphones. If there are deeper coins to be found, you'll detect them!

Because the larger searchcoils are heavier and harder to handle, let's talk instead about *smaller* coils. Used properly, they will also make you more efficient in your coin hunting efforts. With the smaller coil helping you zero in on good targets, you will dig a higher ratio of coins to trash, even though detection depth will not be as great as with 8 to 12-inch sizes. Smaller coils should definitely be weapons in your normal coin hunting arsenal. You can handle them a lot easier too, and they will fit in more places than a larger searchcoil.

New elliptical coils are now becoming increasingly popular for hunting coins. A 5x10-inch coil offers an effective 10-inch scanning path, yet is lighter than a normal 10-inch coil. The new elliptical coils also offer additional depth and are useful in trashy areas since they scan only in the small area down the center of the searchcoil.

Where Do I Look?

First of all, we must always search for coins *where* they have been lost, and we must always search with the *proper* equipment.

But, where to look is easy! Anywhere people have been — which is practically everywhere. Once you get really interested in this hobby, you'll soon have the problem of so many places to search that you truly won't know where to go next. The next few pages of this chapter will suggest locations where coins might be found. At first glance, you'll think the list somewhat lengthy and certainly all-encompassing.

What an impressive collection of coins and other treasures Jack and Barbara Phillips can display as a result of their years of searching with metal detectors.

But, don't rush...please. I urge after that you study my list, you try to recall your own personal experiences over the years and keep your mind open to the many additional locations where you might find lost coins. My list is really just a beginning that should suggest a lot of additional locations to you:

Where People Live(d)

Indoors

Closets and shelves.

In the walls.

Above and beneath door and window sills.

Underneath or along baseboards.

Underneath or along edges of linoleum or other flooring...especially adjacent to holes.

Garages and storage sheds.

Outbuildings, such as barns and animal shelters.

Crawl spaces under structures.

Outdoors

Your own yard.

Driveways and parking areas...where people would have gotten out of cars or carriages.

Doorways...where coins might have been spilled.

Next to porches and steps...where people might have sat.

Porch and step railings...where children might have played.

Around and along all walkways and paths.

Around old outbuildings...on the ground where they stand (or stood) and along the path to the house.

Around hitching posts and hitching post racks.

Between gate posts.

Near mail boxes. Remember that in rural areas people used to put coins in the mailbox, along with the letters to be picked up by carriers. Often, some of these coins would spill when pulled out by the postman. I've heard tales of coin hunters finding Indian head pennies and other old coins around the locations of rural mail boxes that haven't been used for years.

Well and pump sites.

Storm cellar and basement entrances.

Around watering troughs.

Along fence rows and around stiles.

Under large trees...children could have played or had swings here..."shade tree mechanics" might have worked here...especially seek trees with adjacent built-in benches.

Under clotheslines or places where they might have been.

Around patios and garden furniture areas...look here, also, for permanently installed benches and seating areas.

Where People Play(ed)

Fishing piers, boat ramps and landings.

Ferryboat loading and unloading sites.

Fishing camps and health resorts ("watering" places).

Abandoned resort areas.

Horse and hiking trails...especially spots where people may have stopped to rest or camp.

Swimming pools or "holes"...especially abandoned or old ones.

Children's camps...especially concession or play areas.

Around ski tow loading and unloading areas.

Beach swimming areas.

Miniature golf courses...driving range tees.

Shooting and target ranges (but, expect to find lots of shell casings).

Old springs or wishing wells.

Pioneer campgrounds.

River fords.

Bluffs and embankments that might have served as playground "slides."

Abandoned trailer parks.

Beneath stadium seats.

Bandstands, gazebos, entertainment platforms...or where they once stood.

Amusement parks, fairgrounds, carnival and circus sites...the potential here is unbelievable.

Rodeo grounds...today's and those of the past.

Old horse-racing tracks and spectator areas.

Parks...and let your imagination run wild...benches, drinking fountains, large trees, steps, picnic tables, sports areas, walkways...this list could go on and on.

Drive-in theater locations...around concession areas or where children might have played...around ticket windows.

Motels...current and abandoned locations...recreation areas and concession machines.

Historical markers and highway locations that have maps or that present good photographic possibilities.

Tourist Spots

Just thinking about historical markers and the roadside parks where tourists and travelers stop should cause you to recollect numerous other tourist-type places where coins are sure to await your metal detector:

Tourist stops of *any* any kind...wishing wells and bridges, hilltop lookouts, scenic spots.

Below all of the above or anywhere people might have pitched coins for luck.

Near litter cans on highways (but expect cans and pulltops).

Footpaths and resting spots along trails or roadside parks.

And, Did You Think About?

Anywhere people congregate and anywhere people have been.

Around service stations, particularly older or abandoned ones.

Around old churches...where people might have gathered to visit after services...where they took "dinner on the grounds"...where children played.

Revival meeting sites.

Schools and colleges...around playground equipment, bicycle racks...in front of water fountains and doors, where students waited in lines.

Don't forget old or abandoned schools. In the East Texas area where I was reared is the old Steele Academy, a training school for boys that closed its doors before the turn of the century. This is good coin-hunting territory.

Where were the old schools and academies located in your area a century ago...150 years ago? How about the CCC camps and World War II training grounds of 50 years or so ago? Talk to old family members, friends and old-timers. Jog their memories about where people *used* to congregate.

Old highway cafes and truck stops...drive-in eating was a popular pastime throughout the United States for many years. Lots of coins were lost at such places.

Ghost towns...along the boardwalks...in the streets.

Around ladders and fire escapes permanently attached to buildings. As a boy, I recall playing on a slide-type fire escape from a church. I'm sure that I and others lost coins here.

Anywhere cars were parked...at sporting events... revivals...market areas.

Old stagecoach stops, relay points, trading posts.

Bus stops...school bus stops.

Around telephone booths.

Outdoor taverns...look for those with loose gravel.

Around flea markets and auctions.

Courthouses and other public buildings...around benches on the lawn, paths and walkways.

Are you beginning to understand that there is really no limit to the many types of locations where coins await your metal detector? Just think of the places where you have used coins...recall your own experiences. I'll bet you can come up with many locations that are not listed above.

Listen and Learn

There are oh-so-many people with whom you can talk to learn where coins and other valuables might have been lost or are being lost *right now*. Consider this list and, once again, add to it from your own background:

Old-timers of all kinds head the list. And, you may be on it yourself! Yet, let your friends and acquaintances talk about the past and the way things were "then."

Caretakers of parks and recreation centers.

Lifeguards at swimming areas. They can perhaps tell you about jewelry whose loss was reported.

Police and personal property insurance agents can also serve as sources of tips on lost valuables.

Highway clean-up crews know where people normally congregate...that's where they will lose coins.

Clergymen, especially older ones, can give you the locations where outdoor revival meetings were held in "the good old days."

Construction crews...especially those tearing down houses or buildings. Always follow the bulldozers! As soon as they shut down for the night, try to be there with your detector...but, *obey* all safety rules and don't trespass.

Historians, amateurs preferably, who can relate local history and point out where people once used to gather, transact business and play. A common occurrence is for the town sites to "wander;" that is, to move away from where the community was founded. Coins lost long ago won't "wander" until you dig them up!

History books are unbeatable sources of local information. Read *all* those written about your area. You'll learn from each of them. Don't assume that books have never been written about your area. Check with libraries and historical societies for manuscripts. Don't forget the chamber of commerce.

Research Is the Key

This entire subject of research is one that I can't stress enough. You may remember history from school as a jumble of dates and names, all dry as dust. When you're looking at a history of people who lost coins and valuables in places you can search, you'll find that it takes on a new and more attractive life. To me research can be as much fun as the actual treasure hunt. And, it's a part of this hobby that you can pursue any month of the year in any kind of weather.

Many people say, "I just don't have time for research," but this is the wrong attitude. The right kind of research *saves* you time and will greatly increase both quality and quantity of your finds. A good researcher will never find the time to follow through on all the great tips that he can discover.

I know because, unfortunately, I'm speaking from the experience of having more places to search than time to search them.

Always remember to research your own memory. I have often thought about the Harmony Hill "lovers' lane" that was so familiar to young people growing up in my hometown of Lufkin during World War II. Finally, just a few weeks ago my brother and I searched it with metal detectors. I smile when I think of the silver coins we dug there. And, we'll probably find more!

Visit museums and study old maps for locations of promising sites. Spend time at your library or newspaper reviewing the newspapers of yesteryear. Be particularly alert to the "lost and found" pages of yesterday as well as today.

Speaking of Newspapers

Make it a daily habit to read current newspapers with a special vigilance over the lost and found sections. Quite often people who lose valuables will advertise and post a reward for the return of these objects. When you see that a metal detector could find the valuable, contact that person who lost it and work out an agreement for your services. Perhaps the advertiser will pay you for your time or split the value of the article. You might search for it on your own and then locate the owner.

Newspapers are filled with information on locations of public congregations (company picnics, family reunions). In reviewing the newspapers of yesteryear pay attention to learn the locations of old parks and playgrounds, band concert sites, fairground and circus lots and information on public activities that occurred in the past as well as notices of lost articles.

This book is designed to stir your imagination...to help convince you that coins can be found everywhere, but I find it impossible to stress adequately the importance of research.

It's truly the *key to success* in finding treasure with a metal detector. Certainly you are glad to pocket the "profits" of finding coins anywhere. You will discover, however, that the greatest personal rewards of this hobby as well as those of most monetary value come from finding valuable old coins through your own research, investigation and hard work. Even when you come home with pockets filled with coins, you may grow tired sometimes of digging up current coins in the parks and playgrounds. You'll never grow tired of recovering old, rare and valuable coins in places *you* discovered by your own desire and careful investigative efforts. You will only become more enthusiastic and your rewards will increase.

Take Me Along

If your metal detector could talk, it might sing this old Broadway song. And, if you're really interested in finding coins, you ought to listen!

You'd be amazed at the places where you can hunt coins just in your normal weekend and vacation traveling. For example, how about those old drive-in theaters you see along the roadsides? There aren't too many left, and the sites are fast filling up with houses and shopping centers. Still, there must be many coins in these fields with numismatic value equivalent to the cost of our finest metal detector. Deserted highway stops and cafes, roadside parks, camping, hunting and fishing parks can be found along many roads. Stops such as these can prove not only very profitable, but they also give you a chance to stretch your legs, walk the dog or make new friends for our hobby.

When you get off the Interstate Highways in your travels you pass through many towns and communities. Most of these have some kind of park, playground or swimming area. Drive to the parks and let your children play while you search the most likely places for rare coins. Don't forget to fill all holes you dig and to dispose of any trash you encounter or dig up. This may help calm that caretaker who wondered what you were doing digging up his park. Always visit historical markers. Many travelers stop here, rest, take pictures and lose coins. Who knows? You might dig up a treasure cache like the many which have been reported found around prominent historical and state border markers. At least you'll learn some more history!

Off the Beaten Path

When you have time in your travels, get off the main roads...especially if you're serious about coin hunting. The farther you can get from today's civilization the more likely you are to find old settlements and places where coin hunting is good. Why not check out the map before you leave on your next driving trip? Look for alternate routes. Take the back roads, and drive a little slower.

Obvious places may surprise you with the quantity of good old coins they yield. I'm talking about courthouses, parks, community recreation centers and such public places. You may be the first person ever to scan a metal detector over them. But, if you look for leads, you can do even better. Talk to people who are familiar with these little towns...people who can direct you to old campgrounds, settlers' meeting places, old fairgrounds and peddlers' stands. There are always some old timers sitting around the courthouse square or on the benches that remain on small town streets.

One approach is to go up to these senior citizens and ask, "Say, can you tell me where I can find an old timer in this town?" That generally brings a laugh and helps open them up. When they start talking about the past and where people gathered, you'll be amazed with the volume of information you can compile and how quickly you can gather it.

One story I like concerns an ethnic reunion that is still held annually in a Central Texas area. Literally hundreds of men, women and children would gather once a year in this particular location for a rousing picnic that was climaxed each year by considerable drinking of beer and wine and more than a few friendly brawls. Obviously, the location for this annual get-together is filled with coins...and the site is replenished annually. Yet, this is the type of information that can be found only through personal research with local citizens.

Did you make a wrong turn on that unmarked road? What's your hurry? Just drive along and see some new scenery until you return to your proper route. Stop and ask directions. Maybe you'll discover a new coin hunting location that you would never have found by taking the "right" road.

Picnic areas and roadside parks are favorite places for the traveling coin hunter. Search carefully around all tables and benches and out away from seating, especially in grassy areas. Look carefully around drinking fountains, along trails and around trees. Frequently, after eating, travelers will wander into grassy areas and lie down to rest. If areas are large, search places that are shady. Search where cars have been parked.

Churches and Brush Arbors

One of the oldest nickels I ever recovered was found five feet from the front doorstep of an old church. Five inches deep, it gave an excellent signal in our mineral-free East Texas soil. When searching around churches and tabernacles, look especially in front where people might have stood and talked after the services. They lost coins here. Also look around back and in trees where children might have played. Search areas where cars and buggies would have been parked. Old churches also usually had picnic areas which you should try to locate and search.

Never pass up the chance to search any area that was ever used as a "brush arbor" or site for outdoor revivals. A scattering of sawdust, long benches and an overhead brush covering provided an instant worship location. You can be certain that coins were lost here.

As an old friend liked to recollect, "Can't you just imagine some sleepy fellow sitting on the hard benches trying to stay awake and pay attention to a sermon. He gradually drifts off to sleep and, first thing he knows, someone is punching him in the ribs and waving a collection plate in his face. Of course, he's embarrassed and fumbles out some coins to drop in the plate. He *also* drops some coins in the sawdust that are still waiting there for us to find!"

On the Beach

No chapter on coin hunting would be complete without some discussion of searching for coins and other lost wealth on the beach. It's truly the new frontier for treasure hunting, and it's one that is rich with rewards. Any public beach, whether of an ocean, lake or river, is a good place to try your luck.

Sun worshipers and swimmers lose coins, rings, watches, medallions and all kinds of jewelry in almost unbelievable numbers. Why do people wear jewelry to the beach? Why don't they take better care of their money? Who knows? But, we treasure hunters can benefit! It's easy to understand how they lose things. Take rings, for instance. People go swimming, play in the water or run and frolic on the beach in the heat. They perspire and douse themselves with suntan lotion. Rings quickly fall off slippery fingers and are quickly mashed into the sand. An individual generally has no idea where a ring was lost at the beach. The same is true for other jewelry... necklaces, watches and the like. Many people carry coins loose in an open pocket of a bathing suit or beach jacket. Such coins are just waiting to fall out and join the jewelry in the sand.

The best time to search a beach is immediately after the weekend or any time after crowds have been there. Make certain you arrive before the beach cleaners who sweep everything up when they rake the sand. If you'll spend some time with the people on the beach and watch where they play, you'll quickly determine the "hot spots" to search first...where the "bathing beauties" held court and where the "hot dogs" strutted their egos. Always look around concession stands, piers, lifeguard towers, drinking fountains and locations of that sort where people naturally congregate. Try working along the water's edge at both high and low tides.

Both can be profitable. You will encounter less trash at the water's edge, but some very valuable coins and jewelry have been found far up on the beach where they might have been flung by high waves. They remain untouched and gradually sink deeper in the sand because they're away from beach traffic and beach cleaners.

A favorite tactic of mine is to begin searching a beach an hour or so before absolute low tide. I scan parallel to the water's edge and follow the tide out.

A word about equipment is mandatory in every discussion about the beach. Any of the new automatic detectors, such as those in Garrett's Ultra GTA or Freedom Plus Series, is satisfactory for the beach. Remember, however, that your detector must be protected from blowing sand, rain or splashing surf. The danger of water is obvious, but sand can be the real villain because it will seep through the tiniest crack in any detector...

Except for the environmentally protected models like Garrett's XL500 Sea Hunter. Not only is it protected against sand, but it is waterproof in case it's accidentally dunked or splashed. With circuitry especially designed to eliminate ocean-salt minerals, you can't beat the Sea Hunter for searching by the water. Underwater pulse induction detectors such as the Sea Hunter are also fine for the beach.

When hunting on the beach you should observe the same good manners that govern your coin hunting in the park or anywhere else. First and foremost...*fill your holes.*

Let me repeat that this chapter is designed to stir your imagination...to help convince you that coins can be found everywhere. I know that this is true, and so do millions of other hobbyists. Only by getting out in the field yourself — with a quality metal detector, preferably — can you appreciate the true excitement and the real joy of this hobby...excitement and joy, incidentally, that are substantially heightened by the *profit* motive!

Chapter 8—How to Find The Real Thing...

Gold Hunting

Although the "gold" mentioned in the title of this book refers to the general enrichment of your life that can be possible through pursuit of the metal detecting hobby, it's possible to find the genuine article — real gold — with a metal detector. It's not easy! And, it's usually a job for younger, more vigorous men and women than the audience of this book. But, who knows?

It's absolutely impossible to guarantee success in the prospecting field for hunters of any age, but I can assure anyone who follows just *three* basic rules that he or she can be virtually certain of finding at least some gold or other precious metal with a metal detector.

Rule 1 — Choose the correct *type* of detector.

Rule 2 — Use this detector with *patience.*

Rule 3 — Hunt patiently in areas where gold has *already proved its presence.*

These rules come from my close friend, veteran prospector Roy Lagal, who has been successful in finding gold with a metal detector for many more years than we have known each other. Most of this chapter represents his wisdom and experience.

Let me emphasize, however, that hunting for gold with a metal detector is no task for the beginner. Before you take a detector into the gold fields, please use it for many hours hunting for coins, jewelry and easier-to-find targets. You'll be glad you did.

Before we learn how to find gold, however, let me pass on a piece of advice. No, this is more than advice; it's a strong

81

suggestion. Make certain before you buy a "gold-finding" detector that the instrument is also equipped to find coins, jewelry and similar items. Some aren't!

The Garrett Scorpion Gold Stinger has successfully proved itself time and again as a gold-finding detector. Yet, we've also given this instrument a hunting mode that enables it to find coins with ease. If fact, many individuals tell me that our Stinger is Garrett's best detector because they can find coins when they tire of hunting for gold. (Or, when they find themselves in an area where there's just no gold to find!)

Now let's examine Roy's three rules.

Number One, of course, requires the most explanation. What is the *correct* type of detector? This doesn't necessarily mean some particular brand or model...although Roy obviously favors the Garrett instruments which he has helped me to develop over the years.

In the past, as technology and salesmanship prevailed, there were (too) many detector types introduced. Unfortunately, the emphasis on salesmanship rather than technology. Letters such as BFO, TR, IB, RF, MPD, TGC, etc. (to seeming *endlessness*) described the various instruments. Each type claimed to have its differences and peculiarities and, of course, its infinite advantages. And, it is true that some manufacturers and promoters misled many metal detector hobbyists. Unfortunately, many became convinced that they could rush out into a gold-producing area with *any* type of detector and find nuggets and placer gold. It is possible that those individuals who manufactured and/or sold the so-called *gold-finding* detectors simply did not understand the limitations of their instruments. Let's hope that naivete alone explains the situation!

Even with these older (and, often, inadequate) detectors, however, some amateur gold hunters had some success. Yet, anyone who has found nuggets or placer gold with an older detector has seen this success magnified through use of a proper modern instrument. My field testing and experiences conclusively prove the truth of that statement. Today we have the new universal computerized instruments with microprocessor controls that perform excellently in the gold fields, as in all other treasure hunting environments.

Today's modern detectors offer greatly expanded capabilities:

— Detection depth has been tremendously increased, particularly with the highly regarded 15 kHz "Groundhog" circuit;

— Ground mineral problems have been mostly overcome;

— Rapid and accurate identification of "hot rocks" is possible, even for the beginner.

As a result of extensive field and laboratory tests and careful electronic design and manufacturing techniques, detectors possessing very exacting metal/mineral locating and identifying characteristics are now being built. Using these tested and proven detectors, both professional and recreational prospectors are making rich strikes in previously unworked areas, unearthing nuggets similar to those found at the turn of the century.

And, all of the older detectors finally have something in common...they are totally and absolutely *obsolete*. Don't expect any kind of favorable results using any one of them.

Now, when I use the word *modern* in talking about a metal detector I am referring primarily to an instrument with computerized circuitry and microprocessor controls. Detectors such as this with which I am familiar are our Grand Master Hunter CX III and II, the Master Hunter CX and the magnificent new GTA series, the most popular metal detectors ever introduced.

Garrett's Scorpion Gold Stinger does not contain a microprocessor, but it is completely modern in every other way, and its circuitry has been computer-designed. When I hunt for gold, I use the Stinger or the CX III, but under the proper circumstances I would expect to find nuggets with any computerized Garrett detectors (or even with the Freedom

Gold Panning Instructions

1. Place the classifier atop the large gold pan and fill with sand and gravel shoveled from bedrock.

2. Submerge the classifier contents under water and use a firm, twisting motion to loosen material. Gold, sand and small gravel will pass through the classifier into your gold pan. Check for nuggets in the classifier and watch for mud or clay balls that might contain nuggets.

3. Discard all material remaining in classifier. Use your hands to thoroughly loosen all material in the gold pan. Inspect contents and remove pebbles. With the pan completely submerged twist it with a rotating motion to permit the heavy gold to sink to the bottom.

4. Keep the contents submerged. Continue the rotating, shaking motion. From time to time tip the pan forward to permit water to carry off lighter material.

5. As you shake the pan to agitate the contents make certain that it remains completely submerged and that the Gravity Trap riffles are on the downside. The lighter material will float over the pans edge while the riffles trap the heavier gold. Rake off larger material from time to time.

2

3

4

5

6

7

8

9

10

6. Develop a method of agitation with which you are comfortable. Back and forth...round and round...or whatever suits you. Your aim is to settle and retain the heavy gold while letting the lighter material wash across the riffles and out of the pan. As its contents grow smaller, smooth and gentle motions are mandatory. Use extreme care in pouring lighter material over the side. Submerge pan often and tilt it backward to let water return all material to the bottom of the pan.

7. If there is a larger than usual concentration of black sand, you may wish to transfer the material to the smaller finishing pan for speedier separation.

8. Continue the panning motion to let all remaining lighter material flow off the edge.

9. Now, you can retain the black sand concentrates or continue gentle motions to let it ease of the edge of the pan. As visual identification becomes possible, a gentle swirling motion will leave your gold concentrated together.

10. Retrieve your gold. Use tweezers for the larger pieces and the suction bottle to vacuum fine gold from the small amount of water you permitted to remain in he pan. Save the remaining black sand for later milling and further classification at home.

Ace that is so popular with beginners). Regardless of what type detector you choose, I hope that it is a modern one and that it offers a true non-motion All Metal mode and a full range of discrimination for all types of treasure hunting as well as ore sampling.

When you're comparing instruments before purchase, you often are exposed to "bench-testing." Now, used in its place and for the right purpose bench-testing is well and good. And, when you use this method to test an unfamiliar detector, the test will certainly tell you how far away from its searchcoil any particular detector can locate a coin or gold nugget. Yet how many coins or gold nuggets do you really expect to find out in the air in front of a searchcoil?

Through field tests and bench testing, Roy remains "current" with the technology of the new metal detectors. He has told me of one particular detector that performs magnificently in a bench test...coins and nuggets well over a foot away can be detected. Take it outdoors, however, scoop just a little wet sand over a gold ring and this particular detector can't locate it. What I'm suggesting is that you *field-test* an instrument before you get carried away about its capabilities. And, if you're going hunting for gold, you should test it in gold country. Since this is usually impractical, I urge that you listen to the recommendations of those metal detector experts whom you trust.

Modern instruments with their precise ground balancing capabilities feature high sensitivity and can completely balance out most effects of negative mineralization. Hunting for nuggets in gold country can be as effortless as searching a park for coins...as far as most of the effects of ground mineralization are concerned. Gold nuggets can be found amid mineralized rocks with ease.

How about "hot rocks?" Their importance may have been somewhat "oversold," but they exist nonetheless and must be considered. These pesky geologic freaks are simply rock specimens that are "mis-located;" i.e., they are out of place in the geological environment where you find them. Thus, your ground balanced detector may indicate that you have found a nugget.

Hot rock response is troublesome in some areas, but your gold hunting detector will not indicate its presence unless the hot rock is close to the searchcoil, a maximum distance roughly equal to the diameter of the searchcoil. If a detected target is "suspect," switch into the Discriminate mode (set for no elimination) and pass back over the target. If the sound decreases from the audio threshold level, the target is a rock or mineralized hot spot. If the audio remains the same or increases, investigate the target. It has some metallic content.

So much for Rule One. I confirm that Roy's advice on it is sound. I know many detector enthusiasts who have had success following that advice. Roy and I both wish that we could be as helpful on **Rule Two**.

Patience

You must have it. Learn to understand your detector fully and become proficient in its use. Take your time in the field and don't get in a hurry. Try not to get discouraged when results are disappointing. And, if all else fails, fall back on this tested prayer:

Lord, please give me patience, but be quick about it because I don't have time to wait!

Rule Three concerns where you start your search. You must utilize some research. No one can find gold or any other precious metal where they simply do not exist. It's best to confine your searching to areas that are known to have produced gold until you have become very familiar with the telltale signs of mineral zones. And, even when you decide to strike out on your own into an untested area, rely heavily on Rule Two!

There are so many things that are now possible with modern electronic metal detectors! An entire vista has been opened up by truly dramatic technological improvements. Totally new areas of opportunity are being revealed to even

91

the most veteran gold hunters. Novices are fortunate indeed to be able to begin their electronic prospecting careers with the 21st-century detectors that are available today.

If you're interested in finding gold with a metal detector, I suggest that you read Roy's new *Gold Panning is Easy* or *Modern Electronic Prospecting,* which he and I wrote a half-dozen years ago.

Can I really find gold with a metal detector?

This is the question that I hear most often from gold seekers who doubt their ability — or *anyone's* ability, for that matter — to find gold with a metal detector.

The answer to that question is a most emphatic *Yes!* Roy and I along with thousands of others have proved, many times over, the abilities of metal detectors for finding gold.

Unbelievable success can await you if you will use the *correct instrument,* conduct research thoroughly and employ the virtues of *wisdom* and *patience.*

Relics/Ghost Towns

Popularity of searching battlefields, ghost towns and other areas for lost relics has been growing in recent years among metal detector hobbyists. Perhaps this is due to the greatly increased abilities of the new detectors. Perhaps it's because of the surprisingly large prices now being paid for relics. Perhaps it's just the natural growth of the hobby. Nevertheless, when you become successful at finding coins, you may want to expand your interest to relic hunting...especially if you live in an area where such objects abound.

You'll find that relic hunting is not considerably different from cache hunting which is covered in the following chapter. Perhaps one difference is that caches are usually larger than the targets relic hunters seek, such as a single button or spent projectile. Techniques of scanning and locating, however, remain the same.

In the literal sense of the word "battlefield relics" are scarce indeed in the United States. Since the Civil War of 1861-65, our great nation has been blessedly free of wars fought on its soil. Even before then, the only actual war "battles" fought in what is now the United States were those in the East Coast states during the American Revolution and the War of 1812 and a skirmish or two in Texas during the Mexican War.

But, "war battlefields" notwithstanding, there are relics aplenty to be found. The richest trove of all, of course, is located in the Southern states where so many Civil War battles and skirmishes occurred. Encounters with Indians also left vast quantities of relics to be found throughout what was once frontier country. In addition to these obvious "battles" were many other actions of arms that resulted in relics that can be found by today's metal detectors.

And, the term "relics" includes far more than implements of war and destruction. In fact, the dictionary definition is "a trace of the past." Collections specialize in relics from almost every sector of society and life. For example, when you're searching "out West," don't neglect antique barbed wire that is found by your detector. Just a single strand of old fencing can give you a real history lesson when you research it. And, it can be valuable to a collector as well.

What size searchcoil should you use when hunting for relics? You may be thinking that if you seek a small bullet, you shouldn't use the large 12 1/2-inch searchcoil. Wrong! The large searchcoil will detect almost any tiny projectile, button or coin that you might find on an old battlefield. Because you will need all the depth possible when searching battlefields, especially when the battles were fought years ago, we urge you to use the larger searchcoil.

Because so many battle sites are in low-lying or swampy areas, it is well to make certain that your searchcoil is submersible. Don't be confused by such designations as "splashproof" or "waterproof." You will want a searchcoil that can be completely submerged a foot or so...to the cable connector that attaches to the control housing. If you doubt your searchcoil's capabilities, ask the manufacturer. All Garrett Crossfire searchcoils, of course, are guaranteed submersible.

You perceptive hobbyists already know what comes next, but I'll repeat, anyway: For maximum depth and sensitivity, use headphones and set your audio controls for the faintest threshold you can hear. This advice has been proven worthwhile over the years.

As worthwhile as the following advice...scan slowly. Your goal will be to cover an area methodically, completely and thoroughly.

94

Most experienced relic hunters use no discrimination. Here's one reason why: If a valuable coin is lying right next to an iron object and you are using discrimination, the iron object may cancel out the coin, causing you to miss it.

Another seemingly obvious tip is to double-check your hole always...no matter what kind of target you uncover. Of course, you should always double check every hole no matter what kind of hunting you are engaged in. If, for example, you're seeking large objects with the Depth Multiplier, always check your holes with a smaller searchcoil (or Garrett's Pocket Probe) to make certain that no smaller valuables are hiding in them...or that some other target isn't buried just an inch or two deeper. Just because you've dug up one relic doesn't mean that there can't be another in the exact spot! In fact, more likely than not, battlefield relics *should* be discovered in "clusters." They were probably lost that way!

Because any battlefield might contain explosives, take all necessary precautions. Any time you dig into an object and you suspect it might be an explosive, consult an authority...quickly! Remember that many guns are lost while still loaded and that even old ammunition that has been in the ground a number of years can still be fired. Don't get into arguments with explosives of any kind. It might prove dangerous to your health!

A military historian recently told me that he owed his life to a Garrett detector. While scanning in Korea, he often found remains of Chinese soldiers still bearing live hand grenades. The advance warning provided by his Garrett permitted him to call in a bomb squad to dispose of the explosives.

The same need for precaution holds true for underground power cables. If you're detecting to great depths with the Bloodhound, you might occasionally find an underground cable.

Stop digging immediately! Contact the appropriate authorities, and inform them fully so that they can inspect your site and cover it properly.

Research

How can you locate areas to search for relics? Your answer, again, is research...research and more research. Often times, all the research in the world cannot answer the question of exactly what battle action occurred in a particular area or whether gunfire took place at that precise location. Only your detector can prove the locations of battle or gunfire by locating cartridges, bullets or other spent projectiles.

Research is particularly important since so many of the "obvious" locations to search for relics are now located in various state and national monuments and parks where the use of metal detectors is either banned entirely or highly restricted. You'll need to seek out locations about which only you and few others know...perhaps you can develop these by learning more about the history of your ancestors.

Why Search for Relics?

Unlike the cache hunter, who is searching primarily for monetary reward, there are other reasons to search for relics and battlefield souvenirs. Some relic hunters are always looking for evidence to prove history, while others seek significant objects to add to a personal collection. Of course, many relics are sold, some for surprisingly large sums, and most relic hunters search for all of the above reasons.

It is fascinating to read tales of the early day settlers of this nation who simply picked up relics while plowing cropland or discovered them under brush in old battlefields. Those days have passed long ago. Except for those washed up or uncovered by storms, most of the visible relics have probably been found. Those remaining are below the earth's surface...sometimes far below...and can be located only by the modern ground-balanced metal detector.

Just as we advised you to find battlefield sites through research, research, research...we now urge that you practice, practice, practice to understand all that there is to know your metal detector and the way it reports its findings. Read the

Owner's Manual for your detector so often that you can almost commit it to memory. Write or call the manufacturer if you have additional questions. Learn what to expect from your metal detector so that you will know what it is telling you in the field. Remember that your metal detector will always try to signal you exactly about what its circuitry finds lying beneath the searchcoil. These signals, of course, are based on the quality of the detector's circuitry but are regulated by ground balance and/or discrimination controls designed by its manufacturer and adjusted by you. *Your metal detector will never lie to you!* But, you must interpret the truths that it reveals.

Of course, you'll want to cover all holes properly, no matter where you hunt. This is true whether you're on prominent display with your detector and digging tools or whether you're searching in a secret location only you know about. In public you're the example of our hobby, and we always want our "best foot forward." Out in the boondocks you don't want to leave any evidence that could lead other relic hunters to your secret spot. You *know* you haven't found everything that is there!

Ghost Towns

Talk about a wonderland for someone with a metal detector! Searching ghost towns encompasses all phases of the hobby. Looking for caches, seeking coins, hunting for relics...all of these can be pursued enjoyably in a ghost town, as well as the search of buildings, cabins and other structures that were once occupied.

When searching ghost towns, you may one day be hunting in an area that contains only a few relics. Then, the next day, you might encounter an entire town; that is, structures still intact with buildings and rooms in them just as they were when people — for some reason — left, perhaps decades ago.

Any place where people once lived or conducted business will produce treasure that can be located by a metal detector. Thousands of abandoned homesteads, stores and commercial establishments, schools and churches as well as townsites, forts and military installations await you. The list of places where people "used-to-be-but-no-longer-are" is truly endless.

And, many of these locations have never been searched! We have discussed more than once the importance of not being intimidated by the fact that a specific location has been searched before. Remember that metal detector capabilities have improved dramatically in just the past few years and that the proficiency of individuals can vary widely...even with the best and most modern instruments.

To search ghost towns properly you must learn the techniques of hunting outdoors. But, you must also learn how to hunt in structures of all kinds. Never forget that incredible treasure caches have been located in the walls, floors and ceilings of old buildings.

When you're searching a building with a metal detector, also keep in mind that most wooden structures contain a truly countless number of nails.

You can expect your detector to respond with multiple target signals. Of course, you don't want to tear into a wall just to locate a nail. We recommend, therefore, that you search in the Discriminate mode, using only enough discrimination dialed in to reject troublesome small nails.

You'll not be likely to overlook a large money cache!

When scanning around window and door frames, be alert for signals you receive from the iron sashes used to suspend the window frames. Don't rip open a wall looking for treasure until you have exhausted all techniques for peering into that wall by other means. Most wall areas can be visually inspected simply by pulling slightly back on a single board and shining a flashlight into the cavity. Never tear down or otherwise destroy old buildings. In fact, you should let all structures remain just as you found them...without harm or defacement of any kind. Walk away leaving all ghost town sites in such condition that no one can really tell whether you found treasure there or not.

Ghost towns will present detector hobbyists with a seemingly endless amount of junk iron of all shapes and sizes. If you are looking for coins, brass objects or other similar targets, therefore, use a small amount of discrimination. It would take weeks or months — perhaps, even years — to dig every metal target to be found in a ghost town. This makes discrimination mandatory. But, let me urge that you employ all techniques we have already considered...the smaller Super Sniper searchcoil, minimum discrimination, slow scanning, careful study of questionable targets, etc.

When looking for money caches, use a larger searchcoil or the Depth Multiplier. All ghost towns had a trash dump, and these sources of potential prizes can be located quite easily through methodical use of a Depth Multiplier.

Because of all the junk you are certain to find you must develop techniques for properly identifying targets before you dig. Rely heavily on your detector's LCD visual target display to do this for you. And, try to learn more about how your detector identifies targets both audibly and visually. Try to correlate the audible and visual signals before making a decision on digging a specific target.

In areas with lots of junk targets your audio may sound often with blips and other sharp signals as well as an occasional coin tone. If you've followed my advice and are hunting with one of the new computerized instruments, remember that your detector will be identifying deeper targets than others. Consequently, it will give you more signals over a given spot of ground than another detector that is not searching as deeply. You have several options that will cut down on these sounds. First, you can reduce detection depth (sensitivity) to 50% or below and still probably have sufficient depth for most targets in a ghost town. Also, you can reduce threshold almost to silent to reduce spurious signals. Try various combinations of adjustments such as these to achieve optimum audio for any difficult ground you encounter.

What about searching houses where people still live? Provided they are old enough and have enough "history," occupied homes can present many targets. You can look for caches hidden and forgotten by previous dwellers. You can seek jewelry or silverware that was hidden for safekeeping and never recovered for some reason. You can find coins and other items of value that might have fallen through cracks to rest under floorboards or between walls.

Truly, treasure waits to be found wherever men and women have been. Humans misplace, lose and hide items of value in locations where they can be discovered only by a modern metal detector. Of course, never fail to use your eyesight in searching any location. What can be discovered simply lying on the ground or on the floor of a structure is amazing.

When you are searching an old cabin or house or hunting anywhere else in a ghost town, however, you should understand that surface items were probably picked up by relic and antique hunters long, long ago. You will need a quality metal detector because most the type of objects you seek are beneath the ground or are concealed from sight in some other way.

When someone tries to dissuade you from hunting anywhere by telling you that an area has already been searched, we suggest that you answer, "I've never searched it myself with *this* metal detector." Perhaps you will find something that was overlooked previously because either the detector or its operator did not have the capabilities of you and your instrument. Perhaps it will be something very valuable!

Since research is first on the "to-do" list of any competent treasure hunter, you will want to find out specifically where to find ghost towns or buildings and cabins that can be searched. There are many books on this subject that can be studied at your local library or at the shop of your metal detector dealer. Historical societies and tourist bureaus are excellent sources for this information. Ghost town maps are sometimes available.

A Family Pastime

Searching old buildings and cabins in a ghost town is a pastime that you can combine with a family vacation. Perhaps your travels take you to unusual and interesting places...old abandoned towns and mining areas. Can you believe that thousands of tourists travel through such areas without stopping? Yes, even metal detector hobbyists who don't realize all that they are missing! Relics, old coins and other valuable items are just waiting to be found. In many of the areas that especially cater to tourists, you will find libraries and visitor facilities especially equipped to suggest places for you to search with a metal detector. These free sources of information are generally more accurate than hand-drawn maps and guides you receive from individuals.

Don't forget all the many things that you have learned about research, however! Use these techniques to the fullest. Remember how helpful old-timers can be and what you can learn from long-time residents. In many of the tourist areas, unfortunately, you will discover that local citizens are not particularly interested in strangers, especially if the strangers are not important to their livelihood. Some hobbyists become discouraged when they receive little or no information from local citizens or are treated almost rudely. Don't you give up! Good people exist, and there is always the library. Keep looking for "that spot" where you can find treasure with your metal detector. Persevere, and you will be successful.

Discrimination

Modern metal detectors are ideally suited for searching cabins and buildings, even those with thousands upon thousands of small nails. These small, iron objects made searching houses oh-so-difficult for many of the older detectors. You'll still encounter some problems, but the modern detector with precise discrimination permits you to search buildings quite easily. And, you can be certain that you've searched thoroughly!

Because your main goal will be to detect small, coin-sized objects, your standard searchcoil approximately eight inches in diameter is a good choice. The smaller Super Sniper coil may be an even better choice. Because it is smaller, you can get it into tighter places. Too, with its narrower diameter the Super Sniper won't be reporting about as many nails in its electromagnetic field.

A cache that is still intact in an abandoned building will generally be some type of ferrous or metal container. We used to recommend that no discrimination be used in searching for such a prize, but the new detectors with precise controls have outmoded this advise. As indicated above, use just enough discrimination to get you past the nails. Even the cache in a small tobacco tin should generate a signal that you can hear.

Always make certain to let the searchcoil remain in contact with the wall surface when attempting to identify all targets.

When you slide the searchcoil over a wall to pinpoint targets, the searchcoil will sometimes come very close to or in direct contact with a nail. You will hear a small, sharp response, which you soon should be able to identify. Either ignore this response or pull your searchcoil back several inches and double check.

Sensitivity

Many of the early detector models, even with discrimination, could not be operated effectively among metallic targets such as these small building nails. Retuning was a continual problem. Modern instruments have eliminated this problem, even while increasing sensitivity. In the old days, as detectors began to improve we appreciated the sensitivity of the early VLF models, but we had to grit our teeth while getting metallic responses. Sometimes, we'd say, "Well, you can turn a sensitive detector down, but you can't turn up one that's not sensitive at all!"

Now, we can have our cake and eat it too; that is, have ultra sensitivity, along with discrimination that lets us detect most effectively with it!

You'll be surprised at how many old buildings and cabins you can find to search. Just a few points to remember: Never tear down or otherwise destroy old buildings. In fact, you should leave all structures in better condition than you found them...without harm or defacement of any kind. Walk away from buildings and cabins that you have searched, leaving them in such condition that no one can really tell whether you found treasure there or not. Destroy nothing. Do not tear out any boards that you cannot replace easily. Use common courtesy at all times. Remember, you might want to return!

Do your research homework to locate lost and forgotten ghost towns. Find them, and then search thoroughly. It will pay financial dividends as well as enable you to relive history.

Relics come in all shapes and sizes as is shown by part of the collection a treasure hunter in Southern California has accumulated over the years.

Chapter 10 — Dreaming of the Big Treasures...

Cache Hunting

As a newcomer to metal detecting you probably expect to find the hobby pleasant and interesting. You certainly hope to discover a few coins, maybe a little jewelry. And, you know that some good exercise will come your way from it.

But, mention treasure hunting to most folks, and they'll visualize a far different picture. Why, they'll probably think of digging up a treasure chest on a desert island, finding loot hidden by outlaws long ago, recovering money hidden by a man who didn't trust banks, discovering valuable relics. It's *big* treasures most people conjure up. And, that's what cache hunting is all about.

Whether you want to get into this aspect of metal detecting is something you must decide for yourself. I hope you will give it a try for reasons other than the monetary rewards. It's in cache hunting that you must use your brain a little more to research a project. And, working on a cache certainly gives you something to look forward to!

But, remember that cache hunting is *different*...no matter how successful you've been at finding coins or jewelry. Cache hunting is about finding big prizes...and, usually finding them pretty well hidden!

On the trail of a major cache in the Big Bend country of West Texas Charles Garrett takes time out to scan an abandoned building for relics or other prizes.

This chapter explains how you must think and act *differently* when you hunt for a cache. Always remember you'll be looking for *big* (relatively speaking) *money.* True, you'll need all the knowledge you've developed in other kinds of hunting. And, your basic techniques may be the same as the ones you've already learned. It's your overall manner of searching for a cache — from research to recovery that will be different.

Will your detector have to be different for real success in cache hunting? Not necessarily. Garrett's GTA OneTouch detectors and even the Freedom Ace Plus can do a good job detecting even small caches to a depth of two feet or so.

Of course, if you're going for something really deep, you should have an instrument with a true non-motion All Metal mode different from the motion mode of the GTAs and Ace. Some, usually more expensive, detectors offer both motion and non-motion modes.

There's just no question that non-motion All Metal circuitry will probe deeper than any motion mode. If your cache is located in highly mineralized soil, you may need the precise ground balance offered by the manual controls of a detector with non-motion All Metal circuitry to be able to find it.

Unless you're searching for a cache in a building — where you know that it cannot possibly be too far away — always use the largest searchcoil possible. Remember that larger searchcoils can detect larger objects and detect them at greater depths. Money caches have been found at all depths (within an arm's length seems to be popular), but you want to be prepared for extremes. In some areas, where washing has occurred and drainage patterns have redesigned the landscape, caches have been recovered from different depths from when they were originally buried.

All the more reason to use the larger searchcoils — even the Depth Multiplier. This detector attachment, familiarly called "the Bloodhound," is a two-box searchcoil designed to detect large objects at depths several times that of a normal searchcoil.

When searching a farmyard for a money cache, look closely at specific objects and obstacles in that yard, such as a well, the corners of the farmhouse and its chimney. Search inside the chimney and all outbuildings...especially those that contained animals.

Never fail to search an old garden area. Here's where the farmer's wife may have hidden some "rainy day" savings in a fruit jar. Remember that when people buried caches, they didn't want to be observed. It would be quite normal for a farm wife to hide a jar of money in her apron, carry it to some special location in the garden and "plant" it secretly.

When you are using the 12 1/2-inch searchcoil, and certainly the 8 1/2-inch size, these coils will detect objects far smaller than caches.

Therefore...expect some junk. But, it's possible to avoid all that trash! When you suspect that the cache you are seeking is larger than a small fruit jar, we recommend that you use the Bloodhound. An important feature of the Depth Multiplier is that it will not detect small objects. In an old farmyard you can dig only larger and, possibly, more valuable targets because you won't ever be bothered by trash that is certain to be littering the soil.

Bury A Cache

Successful searching for caches usually requires some experience; but it always requires thinking. You must learn to put yourself in the shoes of the person who hid the cache you're looking for. It's easy to understand why a person wouldn't just run out into his yard haphazardly and dig a hole to bury a jar full of gold coins. If you were burying a cache, you'd select a secret place and a secret time to bury it...perhaps, at night during a thunderstorm. And, your "secret place" would be one that you could find in a hurry!

Practice this yourself. Put some money (or something similar) in a mason jar. Go outside your house and bury it. That's right. *Go ahead and bury it*...if only for a few minutes. After you've done this, you'll be able to ask yourself the questions that probably occurred to that person who hid any cache you ever seek.

Would you hide it in broad daylight? Would you just walk out into the yard and start digging? Probably not, because you wouldn't want anyone to see what you were doing. So, choose the right time and the right place to bury your cache. Can I find it easily? Can it be found accidentally by a stranger? Will it be safe? Many other questions will come into your mind as you recover your own cache and relocate it a time or two. This is good experience that will make you a better cache hunter.

When you hear a story or someone offers you a treasure map that tells about a cache that is buried high atop a mountain or in some other difficult-to-reach location, you'll ask yourself such questions as, "Why there?" Why, indeed would someone have climbed a high mountain or gone into a steep ravine to bury a cache?

You'll also learn that hard-packed soil is generally an indication that no cache is located beneath it. Most people are lazy. They would rather dig in softer soil or just bury a cache in a pile of loose rocks.

Try to learn the thinking of someone who is burying a cache, and you'll have better luck finding it. It won't be just "luck," either! Whenever you're tempted to attribute the success of some cache hunter to "luck," remember what the old football coach said when they accused his team of being lucky: "We had to be there for the luck to happen!"

Some of the most pleasant hours I've enjoyed in metal detecting have been spent with my good friend Roy Lagal in the beautiful Nez Perce country of Idaho-Washington-Oregon searching for caches. In the summer of 1877 the Nez Perce Indians were suddenly uprooted and forced to leave their ancestral homeland. They necessarily left behind them many valuable things. Among these were numerous caches of coins and other treasures — some which they meant to recover later; others, which they simply "put down for keeps," which was a Nez Perce custom. Because they undertook their historic scramble to get to Canada on such short notice, some of the caches were buried hastily. Incidentally, my novel, *The Missing Nez Perce Gold* presents in a fictional form the story of our search for the biggest of all their storehouses of hidden wealth.

Over the years Roy and I have hunted for (and, occasionally found) caches with various kinds of detectors. It is truly amazing how much more effective today's modern instruments are than those with which we were so well satisfied just a few years back.

The soil at most of these Rocky Mountain cache sites has a high content of mineralization, and the terrain is generally rugged. The first challenge for a detector, then, is to achieve precise ground balance that permits faint signals to be heard rather than background chatter. Secondly, searchcoils must be capable of operating at various heights above the ground because of rocks and other obstructions.

Cache Hunting Basics

Because cache hunting is different, the basic concepts governing it are also somewhat different than those of other forms of treasure hunting. Following are the primary rules that have proven successful for most of us cache hunters:

— Hunt *only* with a cache hunting detector and the *largest* searchcoil available.

— Conduct *extensive* research; you can never know too much about your target and the individual(s) who hid it.

— Be *patient* throughout your effort, from planning to scanning to recovering…and even after you dig up your prize.

— Never *assume* that because your target may be big that it will be *easy* to find. Sure, some cache targets are quite large. But, they are generally deep as well and, thus, more difficult to locate.

Certainly, we do not suggest that you forget or ignore any of the techniques you have already developed in the use of your metal detector. By all means, remember to use all those special tricks that have proved successful for you with your instrument! As I continue to emphasize in all of my books and articles, basic techniques of metal detecting remain the same because the laws of physics do not change. The rules that were valid when you were hunting coins in the park will be just as accurate when you're seeking a cache in the mineralized soil of a deserted Rocky Mountain ghost town — or anywhere else.

It's the manner in which you apply basic techniques that determines whether you can be successful in cache hunting. Let's consider some factors that will govern your techniques when you are searching for a cache. Each of these factors can enter into successful recovery of deeply buried caches:

— Geographic location of the treasure site;
— Ground condition of the site and vegetation covering it;
— Mineral content of the soil;
— Physical size of the cache (generally overestimated!);
— Depth of the cache;
— Changes that might have occurred at the site *since* the cache was buried (generally not considered!);
— Your detector and its searchcoil.

Misjudgment of any one of the above can keep you from recovering the prize you seek. Experienced cache hunters always make allowances for the condition of the search area and the fact that their cache may be both deeper and smaller than anticipated. Pay close attention to the description of where it was buried. And, when you reach the probable location of your cache, don't rule the site out just because of its present-day appearance. So what if it *doesn't* look like that description written decades or centuries ago! Remember that trees and shrubs grow taller or can die and be removed entirely. Plus, you should never underestimate the effects of both erosion and sedimentation. What was once a deep ditch might be just a depression today...and, vice versa.

Take your time. Be patient, and reap the rewards.

Now that I've said all that, however, let me urge you never to hesitate to search for a cache with any quality detector.

Searching Indoors

When searching for a money cache behind or inside a wall in a house, you can generally use any detector. But I recommend that you set discrimination to a low settings…just enough discrimination to eliminate nails from detection. Even with a motion mode you should have more than enough sensitivity to detect almost any size money cache in all walls, despite their thickness or type of construction.

When your treasure map leads you to a stucco wall containing a wire mesh, here are some tips to help you detect through that mesh. Place your searchcoil against the wall and set your detector with discrimination at a minimum. By carefully sliding the searchcoil across the wall you can lessen interference from the mesh. You may hear a jumbled mass of sound, but you should always listen for significant changes that could indicate you have located your cache.

Walls with a mesh can be inspected by holding the searchcoil several inches or even a foot away from the wall. Getting the searchcoil this far away should take care of the jumbled sound, yet still let your detector detect large masses of metal such as a money cache.

What is a Cache?

Caches come in all sizes, and they're generally dreamed of as a Wells Fargo money box, a big trunk or a set of saddle bags…all stuffed with gold coins, old bills, antique jewelry and the like. I sincerely hope that this describes the cache that you locate some day. In the meantime, please remember that most caches are small. They consist of a tobacco tin holding a few bills or a quart fruit jar filled with old coins. Not as exciting, perhaps, as the Wells Fargo box or those outlaw saddle bags, but valuable nonetheless.

Regardless of the size cache you seek, you must not take a chance. So, use a large searchcoil. There is no doubt that even the best treasure hunters have left deep caches that were beyond the range of the finest detectors available in earlier years. These caches await you and other hunters with the 21st-century instruments capable of finding them.

Perhaps it seems that I "over-stress" the importance of using a modern detector or one with the right size coil. Many failures in cache hunting, however, can be attributed to those hobbyists who are thoroughly familiar with the techniques of coin hunting but are inexperienced in seeking deeper and larger prizes. Because they have full confidence in their detectors to locate deep coins, they may overestimate their abilities to hunt for caches. Since the cache is large, they believe they have all the capabilities needed to locate it.

Imagine scanning *right over* a valuable cache simply because your detector did not have the power or the sensitivity to detect it. Of course, that's exactly what happened to me and so many of the talented old-timers when we used early-day detectors. We didn't even know when we were scanning over caches that still are waiting today for our modern 21st-century instruments!

Research

Most cache hunters spend a major portion of their time in research, seldom mentioning their goal. Successful cache hunters are a dedicated breed, but their single-mindedness pays off in tangible rewards. Of course, not all are successful every time. The beginner should realize this and not become discouraged. If you persist, sooner or later you will hit a cache. It may be only a few dollars tucked in a jar; then again, some treasure hunters have become wealthy from pursuing this fascinating occupation.

Never pass a suspected treasure site because you have been told that it has been worked before. You don't know who searched or when or with what kind of detector! Also, I'm convinced that no matter how often a site may have been searched over the years, more treasures were missed than were recovered. In researching my novel *The Secret of John Murrell's Vault,* my editor Hal Dawson and I returned to a location where — just like Gar Starrett — I once found only a deep and empty hole instead of the treasure I expected. As we reinspected this hole, it occurred to us that maybe the *real* treasure had been buried even deeper, with only a sampling of items left in a container above to satisfy anyone who might accidentally stumble upon this site!

Concerning sites that you may consider to be "worked-over" — just think of all the old parks where coins continue to be found year after year after year...and, not all of them newly minted coins either. These parks never seem to be completely hunted out. Now, consider the rugged, highly mineralized terrain where many caches are found and consider also the eternal question of just how deeply they were actually buried. These caches are far harder to find than coins. Remember, also, that anyone who searched a site in past years probably did so with a detector whose capabilities are far exceeded by your modern instrument.

Never forget that today's detectors give you a tremendous advantage over the "old pros." I sincerely believe that even a relatively inexperienced treasure hunter with a detector from our new CX family of computerized instruments can search out the deep ones more effectively than the most experienced veteran cache hunter who insists on using an obsolete detector. The axiom still holds, however, that a veteran with an older quality detector that he understands can accomplish more than a novice with the finest equipment available.

New computerized detectors such as my Grand Master Hunters CX II and III and the Master Hunter CX (the only computerized instruments with true non-motion All Metal modes...at this writing) will search deeper and with more precise ground balance.

I urge that you give them a chance to help you find big money prizes that have long been waiting for cache hunters. The opportunities have truly never been better! No matter how much skill an old timer had, there was no way that he could possess the *scientific abilities* of our modern metal detectors.

Use the new Grand Master Hunter CX III, multiply its depth capability with a Bloodhound searchcoil and discover a cache that *others* left behind.

Recovery Tools

Since most hobbyists don't get involved with a cache that requires a bulldozer or backhoe, a long-handled shovel is the primary recovery tool. I also recommend a long steel probe that you can use to save time...where soil conditions permit. If you believe that your detector's response indicates a target large and deep enough to conform to the cache for which you are searching, you can probe the spot before digging. Length of your probe will determine how deep you can search. Experienced operators recommend one at least 40 inches long. They have learned to probe carefully to establish just what kind of target they have discovered.

Of course, before you even stick a probe in the ground, you already have a good idea of what you are looking for. *That helps!*

You'll know easily if your probe hits a glass or a piece of junk metal it can easily penetrate. If you find a tin can, the probe may penetrate it to let you know if something is inside. Depth at which the object is found can give you some idea when it was buried. Many cache hunters who use probes become so proficient with them that they can feel a newspaper when the probe passes through it. The real old-timers even claim to be able to *read* the newspaper with their probe!

Low Profile

Most experienced cache hunters go to great lengths to avoid calling attention to themselves. One way to do this is to carry detectors and all other equipment into the field in a backpack. You then appear to be just another hiker. A large backpack will usually accommodate a large searchcoil as well as a Depth Multiplier attachment, along with small shovels, your detector's housing and the other tools necessary for an average recovery.

There are numerous reasons for not calling attention to yourself or any search you are conducting for a cache. First of all, you're looking for real money — 'nuff said. Plus, you'll be busy and won't need the attention of even honest curiosity-seekers and passersby. Plus, if word ever gets out about your recovery of a sizable cache, you'll be amazed at the number of people who will try to take it away from you...legally, by claiming some sort of right to all or a part of it...or, simply, by force.

And, that reminds me to repeat the old adage that you should never put your trust in a *verbal* agreement. A wise man once said that verbal agreements aren't worth the paper they're written on. Also, never leave an open hole after you have discovered something. Even a landowner with whom you have an agreement can get excited about a large hole. Because he can easily visualize it filled with gold coins, you might be in for trouble.

When you are working with partners, make certain that all arrangements are made in writing *before* you start spending money on research and equipment and, certainly, before any cache is discovered. Many of us have had unpleasant experiences, particularly in working with inexperienced treasure hunters, such as landowners. Generally, you can trust an experienced cache hunter who can't afford to have his reputation clouded by a squabble over property rights. Plus, he has handled "found money" before and doesn't tend to get as excited about it.

It's the novice you need be concerned about. Perhaps he simply supplied the tip that began a long and arduous search. Once the prize is recovered, you'll be amazed at how possessive this person can get about "my" treasure. Why, you may even be offered a "little something" for your time and effort in "helping find it!" Don't ever let this happen to you. Get everything in *writing* before you search.

Taxes must also be a subject of concern for any successful cache hunter. The Federal Government demands its percentage of income you derive from treasure hunting just like that from an investment or salary. Similarly, states and municipalities that tax income aren't satisfied until they get their proportionate share.

Yet, who'll know just what you actually recovered out there in the wilderness, much less its eventual worth? That's a good question. Always remember, however, that evading taxes is a crime punishable both by fine and imprisonment. In addition, rewards are given to any individual whose tip leads to the discovery of tax evasion. It's always been my advice, therefore, to pay all taxes that are due and to pay them when they are due. If you can prove that you're in the treasure hunting business, proper expenses can be deducted. Requirements differ from state to state. So, study them carefully; but never pay a cent more than you owe!

Again, my advice to a cache hunter is to keep a low profile in every way. Don't call attention to yourself. Pay your legitimate taxes. Insist on your rights...in a quiet, yet firm, manner.

If you haven't experienced the thrill of cache hunting, you can't know what you've missed. True, you'll experience the same thrill of discovery and the benefits of relaxation, fresh air and outdoor exercise that you get from other forms of treasure hunting. But, you'll give yourself the exciting chance of making that *really big* discovery...the thrill that should come to everyone at least once in a lifetime!

Chapter 11 — The Grandkids Will Love It...

Metal Detecting and Children

After you achieve just a little bit of proficiency in finding coins and other metal treasures with a detector, you will learn that your new hobby will help you entertain grandchildren or neighborhood boys and girls with whom you are friendly. In fact, when they discover that you know how to find coins with a metal detector, the young people will be curious and flock to you — no matter how well you know how to use the detector! Whether you like children or not, you're sure to become more attractive to them when your using a metal detector.

After only a few outings, you'll learn how attractive detectors are to little boys and girls. Children seem to have a thirst for adventure and a real curiosity about how things work. They can be fun to have around and seem always to have energy to spare.

When you hunt in public parks or on public beaches, you'll soon find yourself becoming a veritable Pied Piper with a band of youngsters crowded around and following your every move. Why, to them you're an honest-to-goodness magician with a magic wand that finds money! You can use this attraction to bring happiness by sharing the hobby with grandchildren, nieces, nephews or children of friends. The little people will enjoy hunting with you, and you can take pleasure in their joy as you introduce them to this wonderful hobby.

Charles Garrett

You'll be surprised at how quickly your grandchildren and other youngsters — even pre-schoolers — learn how to use your detector...especially if you're hunting with a one-touch instrument.

Let them turn it on; then, show them how to scan properly. Of course, they'll be in a hurry to run across the park with it. Aren't young people always in a rush? So, show them how to scan methodically and help them to inspect every signal carefully; first by studying the LCD indicator; then, by digging properly.

I hope you'll avoid the temptation to let your little friends become only your "diggers." They'll probably love doing it — for a while — but, it's really not fair. They deserve some of the fun of using the detector, and they may not come back for another day of only digging!

Remember the old stories about prospectors who would "salt" their claims? They'd leave small nuggets and gold dust around to excite prospective buyers who woud then pay more for their property. You can do the same thing for your grandchildren when they're coming to spend the day with you. "Salt" a few coins around the back yard just an inch or so deep and let the grandchildren look for them with your metal detector. It will help solve your entertainment problem because the little ones will love finding and digging coins for themselves.

Guaranteed happiness...for both you and them!

Unfortunately, the attraction detectors seem to have for children can occasionally prove somewhat of a hindrance. You'll encounter adults who wonder just why little boys and girls are following you around. And, sure enough, some children are going to ask for coins or other objects that you find. Now, I don't like to be a Scrooge, and I'm sure you don't either. But, it's been my experience that giving away objects while you're still hunting will only attract more children who might really become nuisances. If you want to surrender coins or other finds, wait until after you've finished detecting.

Even then, you must be careful just how you give away the coins you've found and who you give them to! Remember that offering anything, especially money, to strange children can often cause trouble. The gesture can so easily become misinterpreted. In today's society you'll have to be careful in any dealings you have with young people who are strangers to you. There's just so much suspicion nowadays. I hate to sound like an old fogy longing for "the good old days"... but, it wasn't like this when we were younger, was it?

So, expect children to flock around that magic wand you're scanning across the park or over beach sands, and be sensible in dealing with them. Yet, remember that you can let boys and girls enjoy the fun with you and really intensify it for grandchildren or other young people who are your friends. It's just another aspect that makes the hobby of metal detecting so attractive.

Over

Mr. and Mrs. Otis Rood have enriched their retirement life by using Garrett gold pans as well as detectors in their successful search for the precious metal.

Facing

Because children are naturally fascinated by "gadgets," they love finding treasure with an automatic one-touch detector that is so easy for them to use.

Chapter 12 — Important at Any Age...

Health and Safety

A friend of mine who's a few years older says that he's glad to wake up each morning with a few aches and pains. "It means I'm still alive!" he exults. Yes, most of us in these golden years get occasional reminders that we're not as physically fit as we used to be. Yet, health should never be an excuse for missing out on the thrills and excitement of searching for treasure with a metal detector!

Psychologists have coined the phrase "excess disabilities" to describe what happens when older people minimize their true mental and physical capabilities. They end up with disabilities they do not really have. A classic case of excessive disabilities occurs when Momma dies and Poppa moves in with a son or daughter and begins doing...*nothing*. Within a few months he can no longer get about easily or do much of anything else. While it seems that his health has gone into a tailspin, his physical deterioration is artificial, not real. His loving family has taken over those jobs that would "strain"

Over

Fresh air, good exercise and a dramatic view of the famed Salmon River in Idaho are just some of the benefits Charles Garrett is receiving.

Facing

Before setting out to seek a cache at this deserted farm house with the Depth Multiplier, this hobbyist made certain that he had permission to search.

Poppa and has actually speeded up his entry into old age. The same mental deterioration occurs when the brain is no longer called on to the extent that it had been used.

There are no statistics on how many older people suffer from "excess disabilities," but the number is large. Of course, this waste of human potential can occur any time in life when nothing is expected from an individual, but conditions conspire to make older people the group most at risk.

Old age is often viewed as a "delicate" condition. People tell us to take it easy. Strangers offer to help us. Even an older person in excellent physical condition is urged to be concerned about health. "Sure, you're all right today. But, what about tomorrow?" Age itself can produce a condition called "physical pessimism."

We older people must take special care not to succumb to the self-fulfilling prophecy that "old age means incapacity." Tell yourself that "someone my age shouldn't be doing this"...whatever it is...and, you won't! Instead, try letting "age" be the last — not the first — explanation for anything that might go wrong, physically or mentally. Simply blaming a symptom on "old age" is saying that nothing can be done about it.

Major benefits to be derived from treasure hunting, concern the *health* of the hobbyist — mental as well as physical! Good exercise outdoors in the fresh air...exercise that is sustained but not overly strenuous...exercise under the absolute control of the individual, if you will, benefits men and women, girls and boys, of all ages. And, the zest and thrill that the hobby brings are an absolute joy to the soul. There's no "time limit" to detecting, and a hobbyist is never forced to "keep up" with a younger, more athletic or experienced competitor.

When you're listening — with eager anticipation — to the sound of a metal detector, you never have to worry about completing 18 holes or finishing that tie-breaker set. You can quit any time you feel like it. Scan with a metal detector for hours every day or only take your detector out for just a short while occasionally. Your hunting may be intense or involve little exertion. The choice is yours and yours alone.

Metal detecting is an ideal hobby for us older individuals, whose health permits (or *requires*) light outdoor exercise and who have maintained our zest for adventure. Adventure? Correct! What greater adventure could anyone have than finding a buried treasure...whether it be a 1¢ piece or a sack of gold coins. (Dream on!)

Older individuals in all kinds of physical condition enjoy the hobby of metal detecting. They roam parks and beaches, and they wade into the surf and swimming areas as they look for lost valuables. You'll also find hobbyists in ghost towns and in gold mining areas in search of treasure. For the most part, these people are active and dynamic. They're enthusiastic about what they are doing. And, few generally spend much time worrying about their body or their health.

Some first-time hobbyists occasionally complain of physical aches and pains. Such complaints usually come from an eager individual with enthusiasm who has hunted for long hours. Of course, he or she is going to wake up the next morning with sore muscles. After a short time, the soreness either disappears or is eased out of the mind by the memory of yesterday's finds. And, off they go again! Oftentimes, the discovery of another good prize proves to a better dose of medicine than any salve or liniment!

Incidentally, don't laugh at such novice behavior. I've heard about veteran hobbyists who go through the same experience on the first good day outside after a long winter! Why, at the beginning of a long-awaited vacation, I might have done it myself — and probably will again!

I have been hunting with metal detectors for most of my adult life and have never had any serious physical problems. Why, I develop more aches and pains from using my gym equipment. Over the years, I have developed four ways to lessen the dangers of strained or sore muscles:

• Select proper equipment, including accessories. This particularly concerns the detector's stem...if it is too long you will have a balance problem; too short, and you'll have to stoop over to search. The new detectors are so light and well-balanced that you should never have to worry about weight.

• Strengthen hand, arm, back and shoulder muscles with a regular, planned exercise program. Not much is really required here...in fact, just using a detector will probably develop the proper muscles. At the beginning, or after a period of inactivity, however, an older hobbyist should protect against strained muscles and ligaments.

• Warm-up exercises before each day's activity are generally the answer. Just a few minutes of stretching and other activity to loosen muscles and joints will prepare them for a day's work. Take a short and brisk walk, bend over a time or three, twist your body at the waist while standing erect...these will get the job done. You can develop your own warmup exercises.

• Finally, during metal detecting activities, use correct scanning techniques and your own good sense about stretching, bending and lifting. Take an occasional break. Stopping to dig a target usually provides sufficient break time. Concerning proper scanning methods, don't try to scan while balancing on one foot. Keep a firm footing and don't scan in awkward positions that may put unusual demands on your muscles. Keep all movements as natural as possible. When scanning on steep hills, in gullies or other unlevel places, maintain good balance, take shorter swings and avoid placing yourself in precarious positions.

Grasp the metal detector handle lightly. Slight wrist and arm movements will be necessary, but make only comfortable side-to-side swings with your searchcoil. If you are determined to swing the coil widely, use a method that is natural and one that causes the least unnecessary wrist movements. Let the entire arm and body "swing," and occasionally change hands so that the other arm can manage the coil for a while.

Whenever you feel yourself tightening up, stop and rest. Remember: it's *your* hobby, and you set the schedule. Most likely, however, stopping to dig targets will provide the rest you need. Actually, you should think of your next detected target as a blessing. You'll get to stop, stoop down and dig it up. This activity gives other muscles a workout, which will help prevent soreness that can come from long periods of continuously swinging the coil without a break.

Most important of all, *use common sense and take care of yourself!* There are no "time limits" to metal detecting. You have the rest of your life.

When to Hunt

And, speaking of time...you may be asking...just when should I hunt? Is there a special time better than others? Time of day? Time of year?

The answer to all your questions is to hunt any time...day or night, morning or evening, rain or shine, summer or winter...all seasons are treasure hunting seasons. Use your own best judgment and, always remember, you're hunting because you *want to* and because you *enjoy it.* If the hobby should ever become tedious or boring, give it a rest and wait for your interest to return. Frankly, I can't imagine that hunting for treasure could ever be boring, what with all the wonderful coins, items of jewelry and other valuable objects just waiting to be found.

But, when to hunt...here are some suggestions. Now that your time is truly your own, you can hunt when recreational areas are not crowded. After your evening meal when the day is cooler, you might go to a nearby park or swimming area to search for an hour or so. On trips you can spend as much of the day as you like searching outlying and out-of-town sites. Make it a habit to stop along the roadway at various parks and roadside parks where you and your companions can stretch your legs and refresh yourselves. At the same time, you can search and recover a coin or two lost by those folks who have used the park before you.

Treasure hunting is more than a good excuse to arise in the morning. It lets us limber up and get the blood circulating. Get up an hour earlier than normal; drive to the park or into any public area and search along deserted traffic paths that are heavily congested during the day. Get out before most people do; the rewards will be yours. Any time you're driving along and see an area that looks promising...stop, get out with your detector and scan a sweep or two. You'll never know what you may find until your detector sings out and you dig. The retired government official I wrote about in Chapter 2 of this book told me that he *never* goes for a walk now without taking his detector along!

Physical Dangers

It's certainly nothing to worry about, but if you're in the wrong place at the right time, there's always the chance of encountering trouble of some sort. If you lack confidence in the security of an area, work in pairs. I suggest you never tell anyone, even children, the amount of treasure you are finding. The quickest way to discourage people is to show them a few pulltabs and bottlecaps. They'll suddenly lose interest and even the children won't be so anxious to help you dig. Never tell inquisitive people how much your detector is worth. Just say, "Oh, they don't cost very much; besides, this detector was a gift." In fact, it probably was a gift, either from yourself or from your spouse or children.

Of course, you might find yourself being bothered by animals, but no more so than the same problem you face when walking or jogging.

Always be alert to the possibility of digging up explosives. Over the past half century some areas have been used from time to time as bombing and artillery ranges. Now, these areas are certainly few and far between. Nevertheless, if you dig up a strange-looking device that you suspect might be a bomb or artillery shell, notify the authorities immediately. Let them take care of it. Then exercise caution when digging in that area, or just stay away entirely.

Watch where you're walking! Of course, you won't fall in the holes you dig, certainly, but joggers and others might, if you fail to cover them. So...*fill your holes!*

Many natural sites represent a fragile environment that can be easily damaged or destroyed. Please leave only footprints — not pulltabs, wrappers, cans or other souvenirs of our "disposable" civilization. Remember, a fellow treasure hunter may want to work the area someday. *You may even want to come back yourself!*

Toxic waste presents an increasingly serious problem. Be alert to any area (or any piece of flotsam or jetsam) that looks or smells bad...in any way. *Keep away from anything* that you suspect of being contaminated .

Don't Get Stung!

The above warning doesn't concern buying a low quality detector...that's discussed elsewhere in this book! It's inevitable that people who venture into the out-of-doors may occasionally encounter insects and similar unpleasant creatures. You don't need to be told to try to avoid them. Since the detector enthusiast is out of doors, he should be aware of dangers from insects and other varmints. Of course, the greatest danger from most of these is during the warm months of late spring, summer and early fall. There is very little danger during cold weather. To avoid insects, generally, it's a good idea not to use scented preparations such as deodorants, hair spray and perfume which might attract bugs. If you're in an unknown area or one where you've been bothered by insects before, keep a can of insecticide handy. If you are allergic to stings, follow your doctor's advice.

Use good common sense. Wear sturdy gloves before you set about moving debris and lumber. Look on the underside of lumber and other large objects before picking it up, whenever possible. Don't get under old buildings or porches unless you proceed cautiously. You might want to consider wearing a hat or scarf to keep insects out of your hair, especially when searching in or under an old structure. Always inspect all searching in or under an old structure. Always inspect any areas carefully before you enter them. Ticks and chiggers (in Texas, for sure!) give some of us real fits. Their season starts in March or April and ends in September, with the peak coming in the hottest months. Of course, fire ants in many places seem to have devoured most ticks, but it seems ants are now more of a problem than ticks used to be!

I'm certainly not trying to scare you with all this talk about insects and such. But, it's a good idea to keep them in mind any time you're out of doors, whether you're using a metal detector or not!

Actually, from the standpoint of health and safety the worst things that will probably ever befall a detecting hobbyist are sunburn and getting wet in a sudden storm. Even these can be minimized by sunscreen, proper clothing and following common sense rules of exposure.

Above all, use all the good common sense you've gained over the years! Don't let needless worry interfere with the joys and thrills you'll get from treasure hunting. Accurate knowledge and planning will not only help you dispel unreasonable fears, but materially reduce the chances of encountering problems. It is the *unknown* that we fear most.

Remember the Boy Scout motto: Be Prepared.

Law and the Hobby

A s a casual hobbyist looking for coins in the park or on property belonging to an individual who gave you permission to hunt, you aren't going to run afoul of any laws that govern hunting for historic artifacts or disturbing potential archaeological sites.

I would like, however, to raise just a few legal points that you should consider before going out into the field to scan with a metal detector and to remind you that there are laws applicable to various treasure hunting situations. Each state has its own laws concerning where you can hunt and whether you may keep treasure when it is found. You should learn these laws.

All states have laws against trespassing. If a sign says, "Keep Out," do just that. It is always best to seek permission. Anyway, how can you listen to your metal detector if you have to keep an ear cocked for a returning property owner...or, a siren?

With the proper attitude and a true explanation of your purpose, you will be surprised at the cooperation you will receive from most landowners. The majority of them will be curious enough about your metal detector and what you hope to find, to agree to let you search. Offer to split, giving them 25% (or less) of all you find and they will usually be more willing. If large amounts of treasure are believed to be hidden or buried on another's property, a properly drawn legal agreement is a *must!* Such an agreement between both you and all landowners (husband and wife, etc.) will eliminate any later disagreements which might otherwise arise.

Charles Garrett

Ownership of Property

Finder's Keepers — There may be some truth in this old statement, especially about unmarked items such as coins. But, there are certainly exceptions, particularly when you start considering other objects whose ownership can be more easily identified. No matter what kind of treasure you are looking for, I urge you to have a general knowledge of the laws of ownership. You can never tell what you'll find or where you'll find it! Finder's Keepers may not be appropriate for an object you discover on private or posted property if the landowner decides to dispute your claim. On the other hand, Finder's Keepers generally applies to any owner-not-identified item you find when you are not trespassing, when you are hunting legally on any public land and when the rightful owner cannot be identified. Of course, anyone can claim ownership of anything you find; it may then be left to the courts to decide the rightful owner.

Treasure trove — In the United States this is broadly defined as any gold or silver in coin, plate or bullion and paper currency that has been found concealed in the earth or in a house belonging to another person, even when found hidden in movable property belonging to others such as a book, bureau, safe or a piece of machinery. To be classed as treasure trove the item(s) must have been lost long enough to indicate that the original owner is dead or unknown. All found property can generally be separated into five legal categories:

Abandoned property, as a general rule, is a tangible asset discarded or abandoned willfully and intentionally by its original owners. Thus, it becomes the property of the first person who discovers and desires it. An example would be a household item such as an old sofa discarded into a trash receptacle. If the trash collector (or anyone else, for that matter) decides to take the sofa, they can do so legally.

Concealed property is tangible property hidden by its owners to prevent observation, inventory, acquisition or possession by other parties. In most cases, when such property is found, the courts order its return to the original owner. Sometimes the finder is given a small reward, more for his honesty in reporting the find than for the effort of discovery.

Lost property is defined as that which the owner has inadvertently and unintentionally lost, yet to which he legally retains title. Still, there is a presumption of abandonment until the owner appears and claims such property, providing that the finder has taken steps to notify the owner of its discovery. Such a case might arise when someone finds a lost wallet that contains documents identifying the owner. It is the general rule that such property must be returned to its owner, who pays a reward if he so desires In fact, in almost every jurisdiction a criminal statute exists that makes it a crime to withhold "lost" property.

Misplaced property has been intentionally hidden or laid away by its owner who planned to retrieve it at a later date but forgot about the property or where it was hidden. When found, such property is generally treated the same as concealed property with attempts required to find its owner. When this is not possible, ownership usually reverts to the occupant or owner of the premises on which it was found with the finder being awarded some amount of the object's value.

Things embedded in the soil generally constitute property other than treasure trove, such as antique bottles or artifacts of historical value. The finder acquires no rights to the object, and possession of such objects belongs to the landowner unless declared otherwise by a court of law. Generally, courts divide the value of the find between the property owner and the finder.

Rules of Conduct

Of course, the first rule of conduct for any detector hobbyist is to *fill all holes.* You'll learn that most every governmental subdivision — be it city, township, county, state or whatever — enforces some sort of law that prohibits destruction of public or private property. When you dig a hole or cut through the grass on private or public property, you're in effect violating a law. Of course, laws are generally not enforced this rigidly, especially if the hobbyist is careful in his digging.

In addition, property should always be restored to the condition in which you found it. I have heard of treasure hunters who completely devastate an area, leaving large gaping holes, tearing down structures and uprooting shrubbery and sidewalks. Damage of this kind is one of the reasons we're seeing so many efforts at legislation that would literally *shut down* metal detectors on public property.

Of course, there have always been laws to protect private as well as public property, but only in recent years have these been rigidly enforced to limit the activity of metal detector hobbyists. Why has this happened? Public lands, parks, recreational areas and such are continuously maintained and kept in good condition so that those using such facilities can enjoy them to the fullest. When there is willful destruction, laws protecting the property are more rigidly enforced and new laws are sought. There are numerous methods you can use to retrieve coins and other objects without destroying landscaping and making unsightly messes.

An experienced hobbyist seeks to leave an area that has been searched in such a condition that nobody will know that it has ever been searched. I always urge that any area be left in *better* condition it was found! All hobbyists must become aware of their responsibility to protect the property of others and to keep public property fit for all. Persons who destroy property, leave large holes unfilled, or tear down buildings in search of valuables, should not to be called treasure hunters — but, more properly...looters and scavengers.

Taxes

All treasure that you find must be declared as income during the year in which you receive a monetary gain from that treasure. If you find $1,000 in coins, which you spend at once because they have no numismatic value, then you must declare the face value of those coins in the current year's income tax report. If, however, you discover a valuable coin

— or, say, an antique pistol — you do not make a declaration until you sell the item(s) and then only for the amount you received. If you decide to donate some of your finds to historical societies or museums, you may be able to deduct the fair market price of the items as charitable contributions. Simply stated, the tax laws require you to declare all income from treasure hunting.

You may be allowed to deduct some or all of your expenses but you must have good records. You are advised to check with a tax accountant, especially if you plan to become a full-time treasure hunter.

Code of Ethics

Filling holes and protecting the landscaping is but one requirement of a dedicated metal detector hobbyist. Thousands of individuals and organization have adopted a formal Metal Detector Operators Code of Ethics:

"— I will respect private and public property, all historical and archaeological sites and will do no metal detecting on these lands without proper permission.

"— I will keep informed on and obey all laws, regulations and rules governing federal, state and local public lands.

"— I will aid law enforcement officials whenever possible.

"— I will cause no willful damage to property of any kind, including fences, signs and buildings, and will always fill holes I dig.

"— I will not destroy property, buildings or the remains of ghost towns and other deserted structures.

"— I will not leave litter or uncovered items lying around. I will carry all trash and dug targets with me when I leave each search area.

"— I will observe the Golden Rule, using good outdoor manners and conducting myself at all times in a manner that will add to the stature and public image of all people engaged in the field of metal detection."

Policing this code is an important job of the scores of local metal detector and treasure hunting clubs organized over the nation. Clubs varying in size from a few members to hundreds meet regularly for fellowship, to share adventures and to compare their success in the field and water. At the same time, these sincere hobbyists seek knowledge of new developments in the science of metal detecting and try to remain abreast of the rapidly changing laws and regulations that govern their hobby. I believe that almost every hobbyist — especially one just learning about metal detectors — can benefit from membership in a club.

I urge you to investigate joining one. Call us at 1-800-527-4011 for the location of a club in your area.

Why, you may even want to start your own club! How about those fellow retirees from your old company or the individuals with whom you've been spending time on park benches or in a coffee shop? You'll find some of them just as interested in the new hobby as you, and your friendships will certainly reach new heights as they are stimulated with new-found treasure.

Our hobby — the sport of metal detecting — has been kept clean and dignified by people who care about it, while they express a similar concern for themselves and their fellow man. Most of us who use metal detectors will go out of our way to protect this most rewarding and enjoyable hobby that we love so much...as well as sharing our enjoyment with others. Why, that's one of the reasons that I wrote this book!

Keeping the hobby clean takes the effort and dedication of everyone...not just a few. So, as you go about enjoying your leisure — or perhaps full-time (lucky you) — activity, be professional! Be worthy of your calling!

I wish you success and happiness and maybe...

I'll see you in the field!

Form for Ordering...

Ram Books
Gold Panning Kit

Please send the following books:

☐ Real Gold in Those Golden Years . . . .$ 9.95
☐ Let's Talk Treasure Hunting $14.95
☐ Buried Treasures You Can Find $14.95
☐ The New Successful Coin Hunting $12.95
☐ Modern Metal Detectors $14.95
☐ Modern Electronic Prospecting . . . .$ 9.95
☐ Weekend Prospecting . . . .$ 3.95
☐ Gold Panning Is Easy . . . .$ 9.95
☐ Treasure Recovery from Sand & Sea $14.95
☐ Sunken Treasure: How to Find It $14.95
☐ New World Shipwrecks: 1492-1825 . . . . .$16.95
☐ Treasure from British Waters . . . .$ 7.95
☐ An Introduction to Metal Detectors . . . . . .$ 1.00
   (No shipping/handling charge for this book)
☐ Find an Ounce of Gold a Day . . . .$ 3.00
   (Included free with Gold Panning Kit)

True Treasure Tales

☐ Secret of John Murrell's Vault . . . .$ 4.95
☐ Missing Nez Perce Gold . . . .$ 4.95

Gold Panning Kit

☐ Complete kit for gold panning $24.95
      (Kit requires NO shipping/handling charge.)
      Also, when Gold Panning Kit is ordered,
      no shipping/handling charge for any books.

Ram Publishing Company
P.O. Drawer 38649
Dallas, TX 75238
FAX: 214-494-1881
(Credit Card Orders Only)

Please add $1 for
each book
(maximum of $3
  handling charges.)

Total for items $_____

8.25% Tax (Texas residents) $_____

Handling Charge $_____

                              TOTAL $_____

Enclosed check or money order

I prefer to order through
☐ MasterCard
☐ Visa
By telephone:
1-800-527-4011   _____

                              Credit Card Number

_____

Expiration Date   **Phone Number (8 a.m. to 4 p.m.)**

_____

Signature (Credit Card orders must be signed.)

_____

NAME

_____

ADDRESS (For Shipping)

_____

CITY, STATE, ZIP